DORRY KORDAHI

WIN
BIG
RISK
SMALL

AN ENTREPRENEUR'S FORMULA

winbigrisksmall.com

Win Big, Risk Small: an Entrepreneur's Formula
Dorry Kordahi
Published by DKM Management.
First published 2017

© Dorry Kordahi Management 2017 — All rights reserved

All rights reserved. No part of this printed or video publication may be reproduced, stored in or introduced into a retrieval system, or transmitted, in any form, or by any means (electrical, mechanical, photocopying, recording or otherwise) without the prior written permission of the publisher and copyright owner.

Cover Design by Lex Enterprises
Cover Image: Dorry Kordahi private collection

Editor: Julie Athanasiou
Designer / typesetter: Working Type Studio (www.workingtype.com.au)
Printed by KHL Printing Co

National Library of Australia Cataloguing-in-Publication data

Author:	Kordahi, Dorry.
Title:	Win Big Risk Small: An Entrepreneur's Formula / Dorry Kordahi
Edition:	1st ed.
ISBN:	978-0-646-97272-5 (pbk.)
	978-1-925-28277-1 (ebook)
Subjects:	Kordahi, Dorry.
	Entrepreneurship, Business
	Success in business
	New business enterprise – Management
	Small business – Management
	Business plannining
Contributors:	Santer, Lynn
Dewey Number:	650.1

The material in this publication is of nature of general comment only, and does not represent professional advice. It is not intended to provide specific guidance for particular circumstances and it should not be relied on as the basis for any decision to take action or not take action on any matter which it covers.

Readers should obtain professional advice where appropriate, before making any such decision. To maximum extent permitted by law, the authors and publisher disclaim all responsibility to any person, arising directly or indirectly from any person taking or not taking action based upon the information in this publication.

Contents

Chapter 1	Humble Beginnings	5
Chapter 2	Childhood Dreams — Some Really Do Come True	15
Chapter 3	A Basketball Player? A Hairdresser? The Entrepreneur!	29
Chapter 4	Discovering My Purpose	51
Chapter 5	Turning the Vision Into Reality	81
Chapter 6	The Fledgling	105
Chapter 7	Branded — Thinking Outside the Box	127
Chapter 8	The Rebirth Of An Idol — Stepping Into The Pop World	139
Chapter 9	The Sydney Kings —Chasing a Dream	159
Chapter 10	What I've Learnt About Merchandising	177
Chapter 11	Don't Slash and Burn — Cost Control and Planned Growth	197

Chapter 12	Acquisitions: Seeing The Possibilities — Planned Growth	211
Chapter 13	Running A Successful Company — Bottom Line — Profit Over Turnover	231
Chapter 14	The Big Picture — The World Now Can Really Be Your Oyster	245
Chapter 15	Life Is Amazing! — Enjoying the Fruits Of Your Hard Work	253

Foreword

By Kevin Weldon

Australia is a rich tapestry of people from all over the world, they have all brought to this land many diverse cultures and, more importantly natural business talents.

Handed down through the family for many centuries these migrants, from mostly humble beginnings who came to Australia have many third generations who are now the leaders in business and commerce in Australia.

The author of this book Dorry Kordahi is one of those great Australian stories, son of migrant, Joe Kordahi who migrated from Lebanon in 1975. Joe borrowed a little money from his relatives to start his hairdressing business.

Young Dorry grew up struggling through his schooling but had the enthusiasm for sport, at which he excelled. But he always possessed a natural talent and enthusiasm for trading, doing a deal. Starting in one area and place, moving to another — always learning, always improving his business skills.

Dorry's journey is inspirational. For anyone who wants to get ahead whoever they are or what humble backgrounds they come from it really is the book that will help the reader say I CAN DO IT. Now read it and do it!

— **Kevin Weldon AM**

To my family for their ongoing love and support.

Embrace challenge!

Engage in the process!

You don't practice to win, you practice to improve.

*Enjoy the process and you will find
winning is the by-product.*

Dorry Kordahi

Chapter 1

Humble Beginnings

If someone had told me when I was earning $150 a week as a hairdresser in my dad's salon, that one day, in the very near future, I would be on *BRW*'s 'Young Rich List', I would have said, "No way!" Well, it's funny how the universe works and what it brings to you.

I first wrote about my experiences in my book POWER TO ACT, when I was just 35 because, even then, I felt I had achieved enough to have something I could share with people starting out on their entrepreneurial journey.

And while there is little doubt that, in many ways, I have been blessed, my achievements are something that anyone can emulate. Learning is something we must always do. So, seven years on, I have expanded on those insights in WIN BIG — RISK SMALL, in a way that explains how you too can achieve success.

In this book I will share some insights into how I got to where I am today. At the end of each chapter, I will summarise the lessons learned, using my

'Entrepreneurial Formula' to explain the points and examine certain aspects of the story. These are the features of my story which I hope will add value to you and your vision.

So, to begin, even as a young child I had dreams and visions that were far beyond the horizons of my family's expectations. I believed — actually, I knew with the burning passion of certainty — that somewhere beyond the bounds of past experience I was going to become successful. But, before I was truly able to shine, I needed to find my purpose.

With no higher education or family fortune behind me and armed only with that burning desire to succeed, I proved that with hard work and determination it's possible not only to reach the seemingly unreachable star but to positively touch the lives of countless others along the way.

It is important that you understand a few aspects of my makeup before you reach points in my story where you might say to yourself, "That could never happen to me."

Where there is light, there is also darkness. In this book, I freely and frankly reveal some of the most difficult and intimate moments I've endured in turning my dream into reality. This not only puts my triumphs into important perspective, but it will also — and this is crucial for those of you who yearn to emulate my success but think I must possess a 'Midas touch' or innate ability — illustrate that no man can shine without shadows.

All too often, people view others who have exceeded their level of achievements with envy. They fail to see the undeniable truth: that anyone can realise their full potential if they are prepared to commit to their dream and accept that where there are highs, there are also lows. We may not glimpse the lows in those we admire (or envy) from afar, but they are there. So, before you do anything else, make the commitment to see your vision through, no matter how bumpy the road may become.

My beginnings were unremarkable. Born to a middle-class, close-knit family, I was raised with strong values. My mother stayed at home to take care of the household while my father earned a living. I wasn't brought up with wealth or the luxuries that money can buy. It was more about acquiring the values of respect, family, and traditions. I see now that having those values kept me grounded and humble.

Before he retired, my father, Joseph, was a highly respected professional in his field. He honed his skills and refined his craft, always wanting to give his clientele the best value for their money. For nearly 40 years, he ran his own business; first by running two salons in Lebanon and, later, when he and his family migrated to Australia in 1976, one in Sydney.

At 25 years of age, my father arrived in 'the lucky country' to make a new start with his family. He did not speak fluent English, so he enrolled in an English language course. Following this, he secured a position at a salon in the Boulevard Hotel on William Street in Sydney. Within three months, he saw an opportunity to open up a salon in the suburb of Punchbowl. Even now, he still coifs the odd client, although these days it is more of a hobby.

Two of my younger siblings were born in Australia, my brother, David and my sister, Christine. My older brother, Danny, and I were migrants along with our parents; I was only a year old.

So, what made my parents travel across the world with two toddlers to start a new life in a country where they could barely speak the language? War.

Civil war broke out in Lebanon in 1975. My aunt left her homeland almost as soon as the first shots were fired and it didn't take my dad long to follow suit. Eventually, my father's entire extended family left their ancestral homeland to settle in a climate where it felt safer to raise their children. They could just have easily gone to France or elsewhere in Europe, but Australia was seen as the land of opportunity by many and enthused about by my aunt who had migrated to the land 'down under' a few years earlier. The Kordahi family believed there were more opportunities in this country than anywhere else they might have chosen to migrate. Not everyone was fortunate enough to pack up and leave behind the violence erupting all around them. For example, my mother, Mary, left her whole extended family behind.

I admire my dad and give him a lot of credit for being brave enough to gather up his wife and two young children to start over in a new country with little money and limited English at such a young age. To have the drive and determination to open up a salon within his first year is something I greatly respect. Nothing I experienced could rival what my father put on the line for his family to ensure we were raised in a safe society.

Back then, the area of Punchbowl was quite raw but, even so, setting up a new business took money. With only a couple of thousand dollars to his name, my father secured a loan from his sisters, who were convinced that he would build a solid reputation for himself in his new country. Had he remained in Lebanon, our family's financial security would likely still have been assured as my father possessed strong political connections, which no doubt would have taken him a long way. However, financial security is no substitute for physical and emotional security, so he was prepared to forsake material comfort for the love and safety of our family. For my father and, in turn, for me in emulating his morality, family is more important than money. Money comes and goes, but family roots remain.

One of my more vivid memories as a small child was my first day at school. I remember kissing my mother goodbye and running into class. I was excited, as this was something completely new. As I sat in class playing with some blocks, many of the kids around me were crying. I overheard the teacher comforting them by saying, "Don't cry. Look at Dorry. He is having fun playing." I can see now that this was an early indicator of my character. I did not fear the unknown then, and I embraced new challenges. Looking at the person I am now, I think that moment likely defined who I was. We are all born with individual traits as human beings, but it's how we develop them that determines who we become.

Entrepreneurial Strategies — Chapter One

- Overcome obstacles

- Own the circumstances in your life

- Set your goals and control your destiny

Overcome obstacles

> "Sometimes the situation is only a problem because it is looked at in a certain way. Looked at in another way, the right course of action may be so obvious that the problem no longer exists."
> — **Edward de Bono**

Everyone encounters obstacles in their lives, but it is how willing and determined we are to overcome them that differentiates between those who succeed and those who don't.

My biggest challenge was to face that fear of the unknown when starting my own business. We all have challenging moments in life, but, again, it's how you overcome those obstacles mentally that makes the difference. All hurdles can be cleared in some manner if you understand there is a purpose to them and that there are lessons to learn in every challenge you face.

Own the circumstances in your life

Accept responsibility for who you are and acknowledge your strengths and weaknesses. You are the only person responsible for your success. If you believe in yourself and you believe in your vision, then don't hesitate. I believe that "You don't land on a mountain; you climb a mountain." Some days will bring obstacles. How you rise above those obstacles is what sets you apart. It is what drives you to climb beyond those days and make them count.

Some fear it's egocentric to accept our strengths, as though demonstrating a natural ability is in some way exalting ourselves over others. It is not. If you have a gift, whether it is in sales, music, art or networking, embrace it and use it. It's all right to be quietly proud of it.

Conversely, some of you may not find it easy to accept yourself for who you are. All of us have things we dislike about ourselves. To survive, we must focus on the positives and shrug off the negatives. As long as you're happy with your choices, that's the only thing that ultimately matters.

Accepting yourself for who you are does not mean that you can't and shouldn't strive to make enhancements. What it does mean is that you are positioned perfectly from the point of strength to demonstrate your potential.

Set your goals and control your destiny

Success in any realm requires vision and goal setting. In business, for example, there's no rule that says viable ideas must be accompanied by a 50-page business plan. My business plans were three pages of scribble! Not all business plans are the same or need to be the same. The plan may differ in formula or structure. The imperative part is to implement it. If you don't implement it, then it has no value. So, the important thing is to move beyond verbalising the intent, to implementing it. There are many people who spend so much time talking about what they are going to do that they never make time to do it!

That said, I've always maintained that you shouldn't jump the gun. Although you may have an exciting idea or concept, you must first analyse it; you must visualise it. Assess the negatives in your chosen business and if you believe you can overcome the negatives mentally, then go for it! However, if you can't work through all the negatives in your head, then revisit your thought process. Not all ideas are automatically viable. Working through the pros and cons is the first step to ascertaining whether or not you should move forward and spend further energy on your idea. That's a smart approach in business. If I can't consciously work through those negatives, then I don't proceed with an idea.

Regarding setting your goals and controlling your destiny, well, that is in your hands. It's up to you what you choose to do with your destiny. Believe in yourself, work through the possible negatives and then follow through.

Notes:

Chapter Two

Childhood Dreams — Some Really Do Come True

It might appear as if I was no more than an ordinary migrant boy attending an ordinary school in an ordinary suburb. However, life is full of twists and turns that open up opportunities if our eyes are open to see them. Each and every decision we make has a ripple effect on whatever happens to us from that moment onwards. Even the most minor incidents can play out in ways that are unforeseeable. How many times have we heard of instances where a coincidence irrevocably changes a life? For example, perhaps a temporary delay in traffic resulted in someone avoiding an accident. Or someone who is angry because they missed their flight later discovers that, tragically, the plane crashed.

Coincidences can go either way and, more often than not, it seems too far-fetched to believe such links in the chain are anything but mere coincidence. But what is a coincidence? Isn't it two incidents coinciding or perhaps even colliding?

What are the odds that a schoolboy who worked as a towel boy for a championship basketball team would later end up part-owning that team? The same as lightning striking twice in the same place? Well, not in my world, they're not! That is because when I use visualisation, I actively identify a goal long before it is reached, not as it comes past me. It's all about being prepared.

I attended Holy Innocent Primary School in Croydon, followed by De La Salle College in Ashfield. Always a keen athlete, I played a variety of sports, including soccer and basketball until my father insisted I had to limit myself to one. My older brother selected basketball. I decided to do the same. If my older brother had selected soccer, I likely would have chosen soccer too, and an entirely different set of circumstances would have unfolded. But he didn't. We didn't. Basketball would become a passion, one that took me on an odyssey around the globe.

I played basketball for many years, progressing through the ranks to where I was selected to play for several All-Star teams while still a junior. I continued to play State League and in the ABA (Australian Basketball Association) and participated in a few Sydney Kings' summer camp programs.

Back in 1988, a friend of my father's was the manager of the newly formed Sydney Kings, and I used to hang around with my friend helping the team by putting towels and singlets up in the change rooms for the

Chapter Two Childhood Dreams — Some Really Do Come True

players. From there I became one of the towel boys, wiping the sweat off the court during games.

As a 13-year-old, being involved with a professional team was intoxicating. To be around star players opened my eyes to the possibility of sport as a profession.

My progression through the junior ranks was memorable. I enjoyed playing Division One in my age group. My experience throughout this time is one I always fondly recollect.

After finishing my Under 18's season, the next step would typically have been Youth League (Under 21's). But an opportunity presented itself and instead, I decided to try out for the Open Men's Division One team. I read about this opportunity at the gym. The next step typically was the Youth League (Under 21's). Instead, I decided to try out for the Open Men's Division One team. I read about the try-out at the gym, and I told Danny, my older brother, that I was going. He laughed and said I was too young to make it. That spurred me on! It might seem relatively minor, but it had a major impact on my career at a young age.

I tried out with Tahi Martin, who later went on to coach the Parramatta Wildcats and is still a friend of mine today. Tahi was a year older, but technically even he was still too young for the men's team. Nonetheless, we gave it our best and, after three weeks of try-outs, the coach, Greg Jones, called us back. Neither of us knew if he'd tell us we'd been kidding ourselves or whether the coach had been impressed with our ability, but we were excited to have been called back together. To our amazement, Coach Jones wanted to put us in the first-grade pre-season Division One Men's team. It was arguably my life's most thrilling moment up until that point, and my first real achievement as a young adult. To this day, I can't recall the moment without a smile on my face. To be selected at such a young age to play for the men's team was a dream come true!

We played in the pre-season and after that, we'd either have to roll down to our respective Youth League team or play in the State League senior team. We would train for four hours a night, two hours with the Division One team and two hours with the Youth League team.

Focusing so much on basketball, it's no wonder I failed my academic exams. I trained for four hours, three nights a week. However, despite all the training, dedication and perseverance and having played on the Division One Men's team, I was informed that I wasn't good enough to make the Youth League team.

I was floored. In fact, I was completely gutted. Didn't they realise I'd been playing Division One with the seniors? It's just wasn't possible that I had failed to make the Youth League team. I was fuming and stormed out of the gym. My first call was to my Division One coach,

Chapter Two Childhood Dreams — Some Really Do Come True

Greg Jones. He advised me not to worry about it and said I could continue to play with the seniors in the State League. I accepted his decision, but I was still angry with the other coach.

I have since learnt that every obstacle is a challenge to test the level of hunger and commitment in my life, and to reveal how determined I was to persevere and continue on my journey. It is far better to turn a negative into a positive and to remember that all things happen for a reason in order to increase the chances of a better outcome in life.

The opportunity for me to remain in the State League program gave me the chance to travel through many small, country towns and experience life on the road. At the time, I was one of the youngest kids to play in the State League program.

In our first home game, there were 0.7 seconds left in the game when a teammate was fouled out. The coach told me to get out there. I couldn't believe he was serious. I was still wearing my tracksuit over my uniform and felt foolish going onto the court for such an insignificant amount of time. I whipped off my track pants and track top and was on the court for no more than a snap of a finger before the game was over. That was my first taste of playing with the big boys. Instead of being excited, I felt humiliated. But no one else paid much attention, and I swallowed my ego. Four or five games into the season, my on-court minutes started clocking up, and I began averaging around 20-plus minutes a game.

One road trip we headed to Wagga Wagga and then Albury. We played in Wagga on a Saturday. The Wagga team was in last place, so I figured I could count on getting a generous amount of court time to increase my game experience. Instead, I barely got ten minutes that game, even though we were up by 40-plus points. I was frustrated. I knew the next day would be a far tougher game against Albury, currently in first place. Figuring I wouldn't see any play time, that night I went out with a few of the team's supporters and didn't return to the hotel until 6:30 AM. I sneaked back into the room and dived into my bed with my clothes on just as the coach was calling everyone for breakfast. Had he seen me sneak in, he likely would have suspended me for a few games.

Since I'd assumed I wasn't getting any court time against the top team, I wasn't too concerned. However, as luck would have it, several of our starting five got fouled out, and I ended up playing more than thirty minutes that game. It was one of the toughest games I'd ever had to play, trying to conceal the side effects of the night out from my coach. I couldn't wait for the game to end. We lost. I learned a hard lesson, which is, how important it is to be prepared at all times for any eventuality and never to assume anything as we never know what lies ahead.

Chapter Two Childhood Dreams — Some Really Do Come True

Midway through the season, I grew confident that I'd become an important part of the team. Even then I couldn't shake off the anger at being told I wasn't good enough to make the Youth League. There were politics involved. It was an important life lesson to be made aware of such machinations, for they happen in every facet of life. Politics are indeed everywhere.

Someone who remains a big part of my life and who taught me a valuable lesson, one for which I will be forever grateful, is Leon Trimmingham. Leon was one of my closest friends while I was growing up. We met on the very first day he set foot in Australia. I was shooting around at the Sydney Kings' training facility with my brother when Leon walked in, straight off the plane and was put on the court for training drills. He looked pretty average on the court to my eye. I remember commenting to my brother that there was no way the Sydney Kings would keep him.

After his workout, I chatted with Leon and offered to show him around town. From that day onwards, we forged a friendship, which still stands today. I quickly changed the way I felt about Leon's game as he proved himself beyond a doubt one of the best imports the National Basketball League (NBL) has had to date. He is remembered for his amazing ability to jump over defenders. In my opinion, Leon is one of the most athletic players I have ever witnessed, and his performances definitely changed my first impression that he wasn't good enough to compete in Australia.

I viewed Leon as another big brother. He was 23 years old, and I was 18. We went everywhere together. There I was, a hairdresser on my $150-a-week salary, harbouring the ambition to one day play for the Sydney Kings alongside Leon. Leon became my inspiration. I would often tell him I was living my dream vicariously through him. Even the fans would ask to take photos of me with Leon and mistakenly ask for my autograph. I wasn't the star, but I sure enjoyed the attention.

When Leon left Sydney to play for Adelaide, it was a sad time for me. My closest friend was leaving to play in another state. Leon, though, would fly me out to Adelaide where I would spend weeks living and training with him. At one point he suggested I move to Adelaide, and that he would pay for everything. I was sorely tempted. After all, what an amazing life I would surely lead. However, something made me hesitate. My pride wouldn't permit me to live my dream through someone else's eyes. I wanted to achieve success on my own. I respected Leon's friendship too much ever to take advantage of it in that way. The day might come when he'd be offered a position overseas, and I just couldn't see me carrying his suitcases. It was great to enjoy the experience but I knew I couldn't afford to get lost in someone else's life or I'd lose focus on what I needed to do for myself. I was blessed to have such an amazing adolescence.

I congratulate myself now for being able to recognise how my life could have turned out had I focused on someone else instead of myself. Fortunately, I realised I had to focus on my goals. Even though Leon moved back to the States some years ago, he and I still keep in touch and look back on our earlier times together as a wonderful chapter in our lives.

Entrepreneurial Strategies — Chapter Two

- Prepare for success

- Remain grounded

- Learn from your role models

Prepare for success

To maintain success, you must have the right mental approach. When you think about building a business, you must believe it can succeed and look at all the things that will accompany that success. It might be money. It might be fame. It might be more people wanting to befriend you.

I've seen it time and time again. People who become successful too quickly are often unprepared for everything that comes with it. They end up blowing money on unhealthy purchases and then turn around and think, *Where did all my money go?*

Mental preparation is a critical component to maintaining success and one where it helps to learn from other people's mistakes rather than just your own.

There is no escaping it, once you start climbing the ladder of success, people's attitudes towards you will change. You cannot control this, but you can control how you react to it. This comes from confidence, not arrogance and by that, I mean confidence in yourself and the path you have chosen.

All other things being equal, self-confidence is often the single ingredient that distinguishes a successful person from someone less successful. Make a clear promise to yourself that you are absolutely committed to your journey. No matter how others change around you, maintain your focus and continue to do everything in your power to achieve your goals. If doubts start to surface, take a deep breath. Analyse and challenge those doubts calmly and rationally. If the issues dissolve under scrutiny, that's wonderful. However, if the issues are based on genuine risks, make sure you set additional goals to manage them appropriately.

Either way, make that promise!

Remain grounded

Success is a wonderful thing to achieve, but sometimes it can be difficult to deal with the consequences. Living in the fast-paced, high-tech world of today can make it difficult to retain your inner happiness while striving to achieve. Many important aspects of your personal life can get lost in all of the excitement. I believe if you are humble and try to do good things with your success, then good will come back to you. It's called reaping what you sow. There are fundamental steps to help deal with success well. Here are five to consider:

Step 1: Keep your feet on the ground. It's very easy to get caught up in your success and become so full of yourself that you feel you are above others.

Step 2: Let your accomplishments speak for themselves. When you gain your success, you won't need to tell everyone how successful you are. It will be evident to others without you saying a word.

Step 3: If your beginnings were modest, remember where you came from and who you are. Money has a way of changing a personality. If you have been fortunate enough to have been raised to be humble, do your best to remain that way.

Step 4: Live for the future, not just for today. It would be a big mistake if you only lived for today and spent unwisely, instead of investing in your future. Formulate a detailed plan for how you will deal with your future success. There will come a day when you will want to retire, and unless you have prepared a plan, you may find yourself having to make more sacrifices than you ever imagined.

Step 5: Spend quality time with friends and family. This is arguably one of the most important steps of all. Family and friends are the people who will support you the most. Success can often breed huge egos and arrogance, which can strain an otherwise good relationship.

Keeping good people around you, who really love you, will keep you grounded. Success attracts a lot of people who will sing your praises but not always with your best interests at heart.

Be wise in your choice of friends and companions.

A true friend in triumph is much harder to find than a false one. It takes tremendous loyalty for a friend to watch us soar when we are flying high rather than dragging us back down. Loyal friends not only lend a hand when you're in need; they applaud your successes and cheer you on without envy when you prosper.

Learn from your role models

People often ask me who my role models are. My answer? Everybody. I'm a sponge, absorbing ideas from everyone I meet.

When I was younger, I spent a lot of time with people who were a lot older than me. I loved how successful they seemed. They could have been a national sales manager or anyone I thought at the time had a high position — I was determined to learn from their success. Today, I suppose I have now become a role model for others. Yet, no matter how successful you are or how wealthy you become you never stop learning from other people.

When we model ourselves after those who have achieved greatness, we try to adopt their character, their strengths, and their determination. Their success can lead to our success, and in the process we better ourselves. It's a win-win proposition.

Role modelling is an effective and powerful step in achieving success. It provides us with inspiration and encourages us to move beyond temporary limits and failures. It also stimulates the creative imagination and draws from the subconscious mind ideas and insights, which might not otherwise come were we not so inspired. Let us not forget the most important principle of all. Your thoughts create your reality. Your mindset — what you think about and choose to dwell upon — imprints itself indelibly on your subconscious, particularly if you reinforce it through repetition every day. In this way, you can imprint the qualities of your mentors within yourself. So, select your heroes and role models wisely and let them lift you to heights you might not accomplish on your own.

One caveat: I don't believe in copying people directly. I prefer to carefully observe what others whom I admire do, to learn not just from their successes but also from their failures. You don't want to lose your identity in the quest to emulate. You need to create your own identity. Take from lessons learnt and emulate that which will make your journey a successful one.

Notes:

Chapter 3

A Basketball Player? A Hairdresser? The Entrepreneur!

Although everything I've touched in later life may appear to have turned to gold that was not always the case. In fact, as a child and in my early adult years, it seemed that everything I touched broke!

Study Out — Basketball In

I had finished 12 years of school, albeit failing my High School Certificate with terribly bad marks. Considering I spent no more than a few minutes studying before each exam, it didn't come as any great surprise. I failed to apply myself at all to my studies. Unlike most kids, going to school was not something that motivated me. The only reason I persevered through to Year 12 was my desire to play basketball. Today, people who haven't seen me in 15 years still associate me with my passion for playing basketball. More often than not I am asked if I still play. I never really studied. The funny thing is when I look back through my reports, many teachers wrote, "If only he applied himself, he would do well." Looking back now, I find those comments intriguing and think, "Wow, they must have seen something in me that I didn't see myself."

Clearly, there was some spark of achievement potential, one capable of being either fanned or doused. I just wasn't paying attention.

Back then, my school was lauded for its sporting excellence. The role of a star player on the basketball court came with special privileges, privileges I quickly identified and upon which I capitalised. I realised I could get away with pretty well anything I wanted. If I didn't want to attend a class, all I had to do was to go to my coach's office, sit down and talk basketball tactics. The coach would then scribble a letter excusing me from the class. Talk about being dealt a pretty easy hand! Using basketball as my excuse, I even managed to wriggle out of other sports classes. I was required to choose an alternative sport during basketball's off-season. I chose ice skating, but I couldn't skate to save my life.

After only a few attempts, I was getting nasty blisters on my feet. I hated every moment of it. Instead of persevering or finding an alternative, I went to my Physical Education master and claimed that ice skating was bad for my ankles and would likely have an adverse effect on my basketball game. The solution? I was given

Thursday afternoons off. I would finish classes at one o'clock and simply go home. Again and again, through a combination of being a sports star within our school and having a cheeky persona, I got away with far more than I should have.

The Privileged One

This was my first taste of favouritism. And it tasted great! I remember once being held back in detention during the first weeks of year seven and ordered to write lines for forty-five minutes in class. As luck would have it, the person supervising detention that day was my older brother's basketball coach.

When detention was over, the teacher announced that he was collecting the lines from everyone in the class. As he moved past each desk, he neglected to collect my pages. When he was finished, he announced that he was throwing away all the papers. He added that he wanted the lines re-written at home and on his desk by the next morning and dismissed the class. As the coach had not collected my work, this meant I could turn in my paper without having to do it all over again that night. At first, I wondered if the oversight had been accidental, but I had sat in the middle of the room, and he had collected everyone else's papers around me.

I didn't know whether to feel bad because I'd escaped the extra punishment or to feel good because of it. I decided to feel good! I was quite prepared to take any good fortune that came my way. I was spoiled — and I liked being spoiled. Even then, I knew this sort of preferential treatment would be easy to get used to.

Business Studies Here I Come

However, nothing could magically improve my exam results. My grades were poor; I received a grade of 16% in Legal Studies, 26% in Math and I failed Religious Studies — in a Catholic school! There was only one subject I didn't fail. Although I neglected my studies, ignored my teachers and never paid attention, I somehow passed my Business Studies exams. I just seemed to have a natural knack for business. I loved business, and because I enjoyed what I was doing and was naturally inclined towards it, I succeeded in it. My parents were neither surprised nor disappointed with my abysmal results. It was assumed I would follow my father into the hairdressing business and there was little in my formal studies that would be of much benefit. Even if I had passed with flying colours, I was still expected to follow in my father's footsteps and join the family business. From Year 10 onwards, my teachers made their disappointment evident, especially those who saw the potential lurking beneath the surface of this wayward student. I have no regrets, although I'd never encourage anyone else to ignore the importance of school.

Chapter 3   A Basketball Player? A Hairdresser? The Entrepreneur!

I'm convinced that my story played out the way it was intended and I choose to continue to move forward past any obstacles, ensuring that the lessons have been learnt and not repeated.

I am a firm believer that, no matter what you may achieve in school, the experiences outside of your academic arena are also vital to groom you for the future. I feel fortunate to have been exposed to plenty of life's lessons through my sport and, as a result, found myself more open to identifying opportunities when they arose. Most of my fellow students weren't exposed to the things I was and therefore only saw life through the blinkers that the establishment insists upon. No doubt there are plenty of parents who might want to tear their hair out reading about my antics during my school years, particularly as, despite them, I went on to achieve success.

History is studded with examples of notable role models who flunked high school. Michael Jordan was cut from his high school basketball team; even Albert Einstein struggled with French at school. This is not intended to denigrate the value of a formal education or to encourage anyone to drop out of his or her studies merely because some past success stories didn't start with a sound academic background. A sound education can provide a platform for a future with greater possibilities. I speak only of my personal experiences merely to give you a better understanding as to how and why I chose the direction in which I took my life. The fact is that I did indeed flunk high school, yet succeeded without any formal education. In hindsight, I believe my lack of formal education may have enabled me to overlook the risks and enhanced my professional outlook. Eventually, with my business, I was successful because I created a fresh approach. I've dealt with lots of people with degrees, and most of them think the same way. They have all been taught to think 'inside the box' when it comes to concepts like marketing. My lack of educational structure permits me to think 'outside the box' because I was not taught what the box actually is.

Common Sense Is Not Common

Of course, being closely involved with sporting individuals and mixing with people older than me exposed me to risks that could easily have led me down a path of destruction. From the age of 16, I was hanging out in nightclubs with people many years my senior, and that is when I first witnessed the destructive force of illicit drugs. Sadly, there are so many examples of people not being able to handle sudden adulation at a very early age, but for me, it proved a valuable lesson to observe them and learn what not to do.

I have always maintained that common sense is not that common at all, but I try to live by it. Common sense is simple to follow. Even today, when my success has brought me into contact with numerous people who offer me drinks or drugs simply because they want to take advantage, I still take the same view. Again, it is impossible, even if I wanted to, which I don't, to stay up every night, get wasted and then expect to be in the office early the next day to run my company. That said, I do know how to enjoy myself and the numerous advantages that success brings.

I thank my parents for instilling these qualities in me. They taught me to believe in myself first and foremost, so I never felt the demands of peer pressure as kids so often do.

Integrity is the foundation of character and is necessary to accomplish goals with strength, conviction, and dignity. Giving in to peer pressure is taking the easy way out. Standing up for one's beliefs in the face of such peer pressure is the lesson we all ideally learn and pass on to our children.

The Family Business — Hairdressing A Close Shave

As I said previously, aside from my burning desire to play basketball, it was taken for granted that once I left school, I would work in my father's hairdressing business. There was no real discussion about it. I was no scholar. I displayed no desire to go to university or college, so it seemed the only thing to do. My father wanted me to take over the family business. After four years, I completed my apprenticeship, cutting and styling hair until I was 21.

Thinking back now, it is hard for me to reconcile the person I am today with the one who spent his days in a salon, cutting and styling hair.

Hairdressing as a career wasn't for me although I wasn't half bad at it. It doesn't take a degree in psychology to understand that hairdressing lacked appeal for a young man with big dreams. I wasn't driven by it so, like school, I didn't apply myself. However, I did make some effort for my family's sake.

During my hairdressing days, I decided to get a Visa card with a $1,000 limit. I don't know how I managed to get such a limit on my weekly income of $150. I was excited and thought I could buy things even if I didn't have the cash to pay for it. Little did I know that the interest was mounting on my easy spending; I struggled to pay the card off, but luckily for me, my Dad came to the rescue. He paid off the debt, which was around $800. He then told me to cut the card and not to use it again. From that day onwards, I have never put myself in debt and realised a very important lesson: if you don't have the money, don't spend it. I was fortunate that my Dad was there, and I made sure I learned from this experience.

Despite my father's initial frustration and disappointment, today he couldn't be happier that

I chose the path I did. Instead of spending my days without passion, I elected to pursue my dreams. When I was shampooing and cutting, I dreamt about making money — serious money. I wanted the nice house, the nice car and, most of all, the freedom to be myself and to be respected for being that person. Every day I would visualise myself having these things that I wanted so badly. I knew in my heart that if I could see it, then I would make it happen. Today that may seem passé with the saturation of publications like *The Secret*. Remember, however, that this was more than a decade before the publication of that book and such creative visualisations were, to my knowledge, far from commonplace.

I didn't know how I was going to do it or how I was going to get there, but I knew I was going to get there. I knew that, if I could achieve it mentally and subconsciously, then I could make it happen physically. I'm living proof of that now.

It's In Your Genes

I agree that no man is an island and, again, I credit my family upbringing for instilling me with high moral standards and discipline (Well, except in school studies!). I also credit them for moulding my character and beliefs. While I was growing up, I yearned for the finer things in life, to achieve success, yet they were intangible — I wasn't even sure how to define those things.

As one of the best basketball players in the world, Michael Jordan was a hero to me. I watched documentaries about him where he stated, "I just knew I would be the best at what I did." Even when he didn't make his college team, he said he always knew eventually he would be the best in the world. When I heard that, it resonated. I was determined to reach my goals. I didn't realise it at the time but what I took away from those documentaries was a motto I live by every day now to 'believe in myself.' I always believed I would have what I wanted, even if I didn't know how I was going to get it. I didn't even know what my calling was; I just trusted that I would find it.

Therein lies what I hope every reader will take away from my story: believe in yourself and nothing is impossible. If you don't know what it is yet that inflames you with passion, don't wait until you discover it to begin believing in yourself. Start believing in yourself now, and the rest will follow. Visualise your success, your achievements, and trust that the path will appear before you. Remember the message of chapter one, to always be alert for opportunity. Having faith in yourself will enhance your awareness of life's chances. Visualise all the trappings that go along with the success you desire. See yourself driving that dream car — inhale the scent of that new leather; admire the colour; notice all the people marvelling at your vehicle as you drive by.

Chapter Three | **A Basketball Player? A Hairdresser? The Entrepreneur!**

I had some false starts before I discovered what my true calling was, but my end vision was always clear. At first, I assumed I'd be a hairdresser. Later, I was convinced I would be a star basketball player. In both cases I was wrong. Only now, standing on the other side, can I see how true and how powerful that belief in oneself is and how empowering the visualisation of owning one's dream can be. Picture the end result, and you'll find the road to take you there.

So, you ask, how did I begin to connect the dots?

Entrepreneurial Strategies — Chapter Three

- Find your true calling

- Believe in yourself

- Learn from other people's mistakes

Find your true calling

Look around you. How many of the people you know are unhappy in their work and dissatisfied with their lot? This is because they have never sat down and dealt honestly and openly with themselves. We all have some form of inner talent and ability; the key is to recognise it, to identify it and use it. People often enter the workforce like automatons, doing work that other people design.

Their goals are those that other people have set. Is it any wonder then that, over time, these people who are not following their true callings begin to feel helpless? They feel that there is nothing they can do to change things because they're waiting for someone else to tell them how to change things. Essentially the present and future of their lives will be dictated by the circumstances of their employment.

Your aim in life should be to become everything you are capable of becoming, to enjoy full self-expression of your talents and abilities. Your job is to develop yourself to the point where every day is a source of joy and satisfaction. Success comes from excelling at what you do, and it's difficult to excel if you have no passion. The market rewards excellent performance with excellent compensation. Average performance yields average compensation. Below-average performance generates nothing more than below-average compensation. Which would you prefer?

It's important to note that excellence is a lifetime journey, not a destination. You don't get there and then get to relax. If you do, it will slip out of your grasp. The only thing that doesn't change is change. What constitutes excellence today will be different tomorrow and very different next year and the year after. Just look at the steady progress of technology if you don't believe me. You cannot rest on your laurels!

The joy in finding your true calling is that nothing but the best will do from that moment on. You will go any distance, pay any price and overcome any obstacle to obtain the excellence you now desire so passionately. You will drive yourself with that excitement to begin the day a little earlier, work a little harder, and stay a little later.

Over the years, people continue to wonder what they can do to be more successful. In almost every case, they are working in jobs that they don't like, for bosses they don't particularly respect, producing or selling products or services to customers they don't care about. They convince themselves that, if they just hang in there a little longer, the clouds will part and everything will get better. A pretty passive attitude, isn't it? You are where you are and who you are because of the choices you have made. Nobody can change your situation for you. If you don't have the drive and desire to excel at what you're doing now, it's likely you're in the wrong profession. It's time to look within.

Believe in yourself

To be successful, you must believe in yourself. You must have faith that your theories and your philosophies are right. But how do you know what is right and what is wrong? It's not as difficult as it might sound. What works for you, works for you. Many individuals start companies in unorthodox ways; there's no right or wrong way. If you have something you believe in, just do it. Don't base your life on the expectation of others. What you expect of yourself is often a higher goal and far worthier of your focus. If you need to write a business plan to find investors or sell a business, just do it. Do it the way you need it to be done. Don't get bogged down thinking that you need to dress a certain way to fit into a meeting, or that the business plan must be 50 pages to be impressive. You define the parameters.

If you are in a start-up business, think as an individual. Keep fast to your convictions. If you imitate other people because you feel you must, then you've traded in your individuality, what sets your business apart, just to fit in and be like everyone else. Having done things my own way, I know this to be true. So, believe in yourself and follow through with your dream in your way.

There may be days when you wake up to discover things aren't the way you had hoped they would be. That's when you have to tell yourself that things will get better. There are times when people disappoint you and let you down. But those are the times when you must remind yourself to trust your judgments and opinions, to keep your life focused on believing in yourself. There will be challenges to face and changes to make in your life, and it is up to you to accept them. Keep constant in the direction you know is right for you. It may not be easy at times, but in those times of struggle, you will find a stronger sense of who you are. So, when days come that are filled with frustration and unexpected responsibilities, remember to believe in yourself and all you want your life to be, because these challenges and changes are what can hone your drive to attain the goals that you know are true for you.

Try these techniques to succeed in whatever field you choose:

- Learn how to make decisions based on your experiences. If you don't make your own decisions, you will never be truly successful.

- Set goals. When you set goals, you establish control.

- Recognise and celebrate when you achieve each goal. It will build your self-confidence.

- Consider the reasons you failed but don't punish yourself for them. Everyone experiences failure from time to time. If you learn from it, you are that much more likely to succeed the next time.

- Use realistic expectations to gauge your success.

- Listen to critics but never let them convince you that you are less than you are. Question their motivation. Some critics will tear you down to make themselves look bigger and better, while others will offer critical advice to help you improve yourself.

- Give your time and energy to others. It generates positive feedback and respect. These are the building blocks for self-respect, which are essential to believing in one's self. Believe in yourself, and you will achieve your best. Don't let people knock you down. If someone says you can't do something, don't accept it without question. Don't dismiss it either. Analyse why they say something won't work. Learn from other people's mistakes. In my experience, common sense is, more often than not, uncommon. The general idea is that we must learn from our mistakes. I say there is no reason that we cannot learn from other people's mistakes instead! The internet, books, magazines and business networks are filled with case studies for the small business owner to learn from so they do not have to make the same mistakes before understanding a concept or how a strategy will or will not work.

Analyse how to avoid incorporating the same failed elements into your business. Here are some examples of famous mistakes made by some very prominent businesses. Apply the lessons from these examples to your business and leverage their blunders into your success.

Case Study 1

Borders Books (Australia) until recently boasted some of the largest bookstores in Australia. The company was founded in Ann Arbor, Michigan by two book-loving brothers and became an American institution, with over 400 stores.

The 33 Australian stores, provided comfortable chairs in which to sit and Gloria Jean's coffee and food was available to drink and eat. What they did not provide was any specialist sales staff who understood the company's core business of books.

This flowed from the board of REDgroup Retail (who bought the company from K-Mart USA which had instigated its decline and wanted rid of it). One former Borders executive witheringly referred to the Kmart management as "The grocery guys."

REDgroup Retail was a hedge fund and like all hedge funds demanded fast returns from the highly-leveraged operation.

There were no booksellers, publishers, editors or anyone who knew about online selling or electronic books. Ironically, REDgroup Retail also owned Angus and Robertson in Australia and Whitcoulls in New Zealand, all of which competed for slightly different markets in the book arena. Like Kmart before them, REDgroup Retail wanted to entirely commoditise all its operations and include large, non-book areas. Books were to be sold like cans of baked beans.

Yet despite having nearly 200 bookstores, their brands commanded just 20% of the entire Australian market. Rival Dymocks, with only about 65 stores had another 11% and the remaining 69% was controlled by about 2000 independent booksellers.

Therein was the crux of the matter. Books are highly specialised, subject to trends and zeitgeist that require a huge amount of inherent knowledge on the part of the people who buy and sell them.

With the exception of textbooks, books are an entirely discretionary purchase spread across a host of genres and subjects with completely subjective buyers. Moreover, the target market runs from toddlers who are read to by their parents, to retirees, all with entirely different tastes and incomes. The result of the Kmart/REDgroup decisions was akin to MacDonald's trying to run fine dining restaurants with concomitant results.

The lesson here: know your target market inside out. If you see it needs experts, either learn fast or hire some.

Case Study 2

Once upon a time, there was a phone company called Nokia, which by the early 2000's was one of the most successful brands on the planet. Yet, despite being an enormously successful company known for its technical excellence, in 2014, it was forced to sell its phone business to Microsoft having lost over US$5.3 billion in a little more than two years.

Microsoft paid around US$7.9 billion for the Finnish company, but by 2015 had to write down the value of the company by US$7.6 billion — essentially a US$15.5 billion loss in a single year and a staggering, total loss of close to US$21 billion in three.

The fundamental cause of these monumental losses dated back to 1996, when Nokia prototyped their first smartphone. It was technologically brilliant yet not acted upon until almost eight years later. By that time a certain Steve Jobs was already thinking about the design of what was to become the most popular phone on the planet. Moreover, he launched the iPhone 2G just three years later!

What wowed virtually the whole planet was that here was a not just a new model, but a product utterly reconceived.

No keyboard, just a simple touch screen held in heart-stopping, minimalist design!

That year Apple turned over US$232 billion.

The lesson here: be careful with risk-taking but not to the point of arrogance and lack of impetus. Nokia dominated the mobile phone market in 2007, but in that same year Apple revolutionised it and took it from them. Be constantly aware of your market and competitors.

Case Study 3

Starbucks in the US is a big deal. It has been run for most of the time by the billionaire, Howard Schultz, and by 2017 it had 24,000 stores in over 70 countries. So, you would think that conquering the tiny (by global standards) Australian market would be simple for them.

But there is something in their very name that should have sent shivers up their spine. Because, according to their own website, Starbucks is named after a character in the great American classic, Moby Dick.

Moby Dick is the tale of insane captain Ahab who will listen to none around him, especially his loyal, first mate Starbuck and goes in pursuit of a whale like no other, eventually bringing about his own death and all but one aboard his ship.

Starbucks opened in Australia in 2000 at the same time when Howard Schultz relinquished his role of CEO and crowned himself both Chairman and Global Strategist.

Perhaps the title went to his head? Whatever the reason, he, like Ahab, failed to listen to people telling him that Australian coffee drinkers are comprised of people from more than 300 different ethnic backgrounds. They are also highly discerning gourmands of the bean and grind who are not overly partial to things like weak, sweet frappuccinos.

Rushing to open around 100 company-owned stores, Starbucks appears to have done no market analysis whatsoever. It was push-button, American-style coffee in a country that is full of boutique cafes many of which are run by world-class baristas.

In fact, from the moment they opened the doors of their first Australian store to when they hauled anchor and ass back to the States in 2014, they lost in excess of US$140 million. Eventually, they handed the brand over to the Withers Group, which runs 7-Eleven in Australia.

By April 2017 Schultz had stepped down from the company entirely.

The lesson here: Just because you are successful in one market, never take for granted that you will be in another. Do your research, it's cheaper and a lot less painful than failure.

These are just a few examples of the hundreds of learning opportunities big businesses present small business owners every day. By constructively studying everything that isn't working in the world of business and relating it back to your business, you can eliminate many of the costly mistakes your business might otherwise make. Thank the Borders, Nokias, Microsofts and Starbucks of the world for making your business choices easier and saving you money!

Notes

Chapter 4

Discovering My Purpose

If your eyes are open and your spirit is willing, opportunities in life can come from anywhere — even the most unlikely sources. Train yourself to be consciously aware of everything that is happening around you including every word that is spoken, every action that occurs and every encounter you experience. Something as innocuous as overhearing a conversation about how a widget could be that much better if only it offered an XYZ component can generate in you an inspired thought — an idea that might easily become the next Spanx or Airbnb. Think of just how simple those inventions really are and the money they made their inventors after they hit the market. It might not be an actual invention; it could be an idea that fills a niche for a service not currently provided. It might be that you learn of a business that would benefit from someone with your particular skill set.

Hey Try This

Ideas come to us at the strangest times. Ever find yourself looking at a sunset when suddenly a little voice inside you says, "Hey, what about trying your hand at…?" If you never listen, if you never try, you'll never know. If your mind is closed to that little voice, if your eyes are blinkered to what is happening around you, if your ears are not attuned to listen to what people are saying, opportunities are passing you by, unnoticed.

When I was 16 years old, I began working for my cousin, George, in the shoe department of his sports store. I discovered I was a natural at sales because I love talking with people. George later moved on to start up a business he named ICM, selling t-shirts and polo shirts wholesale. Later, my older brother, Danny, joined him. By this time, I was working for my father in the hairdressing business. When I turned 21, George took me aside and said, "Listen, I'd like you to work with me in sales. Will you think about it?" I did think about it. I thought, yes, I'd like to be someone who wears a suit to work every day. I'd like to feel like a real businessperson, someone who goes out to negotiate deals and hold meetings. I've always desired that. My dad didn't want to lose me, so, I decided I'd work for George Monday to Friday and continue working for my father on weekends. This gave me the chance to dip my toe in the world of sales without relinquishing my hold on my existing career.

From the very first day, I felt a shiver of excitement. I knew sales was where my future lay, a field where I could make a successful career for myself. "I will do this for a very long time," I said to myself. "This is going to give me what I need to achieve my dreams." And it has. After all this time, I am still in sales and still loving it. I have progressed, I have made a lot of money, and I have created a lot of opportunities, but it was more than that. I felt in my gut that sales was my calling that this was going to be my break. All because I was open to what was going on around me because I listened to that little voice. No earth-shattering occurrence out of my control dramatically spun my life in a different direction. Someone simply pointed out a new path and I thought, *Why not?* I made a choice to take those first few steps.

George's business at that stage was focused on wholesaling polo and t-shirts. The products were purchased plain to sell to companies who then would print them up with their own designs and sell them to their corporate clients. When I began working there, I was thrown into the deep end. I knew next to nothing about garments or weight or fabric, let alone industry terminology. One of my first meetings was with a potential customer who brought along one of his sales people. My brother told me to just, "Make it up as you go along if you have to." He threw me an 180-gram t-shirt and said, "Go sell it." I walked into the meeting and bluffed my way through as best I could. Even though the client had easily 15 years of industry experience, he left with the impression that I knew my stuff — even though I didn't. He even commented on the fact that I seemed to know a fair bit about the product although I was fairly young. I claimed that I'd just learned as I went along.

At the age of 21, I had found my niche in the sales arena, and I was immediately convinced of my abilities. Eventually, Dad accepted that I wouldn't be taking over his business and, thankfully, he didn't try to force the issue. He did, however, implore my cousin to convince me that I would do better running my own business than I would selling for someone else. I like to think that my father enjoyed a wry smile when, three years later, I left my cousin's business to play professional basketball in Lebanon. Likely he may have even felt a sense of relief, as my brother and I both working for our cousin had led to some tense moments of sibling rivalry.

Looking back, I remember the fights my brother and I had as if they were yesterday. I wasn't willing to listen and Danny wasn't willing to let me run off like a loose cannon adopting my own philosophies, so of course, we clashed. Danny was already working in the company when I started, and while most of the fights arose because he was older than me and wanted me to do exactly as he said, the fact was I excelled in sales without taking his advice. Eighteen months down the track, George's sister, Lina, wanted to start up a merchandise business. George asked me to help her. I was more than a bit disappointed and even nervous about going into a start-up company. I felt I'd earned the right to stay with George and Danny, but they were merging their business with two other companies. They both knew it would give an extremely bad impression to their new partners if they witnessed the Kordahi brothers constantly at each other's throats. In essence, I was fired, and I felt sick about it. I knew I was lucky to have been offered an alternative, but I was upset and angry at being pushed out. Having said that, part of me was secretly pleased because with the new business would be new challenges and I do like to test myself, even if it did mean moving out of comfortable surroundings.

Lina had started running her new company, Deep, from her bedroom in Clovelly, with no clients. I was 23. I was given what, in those days, was every cold caller's Bible — the Yellow Pages. Lina told me there were a wealth of clients in that book and to pick a section, start calling and try to sell our services. It was a tough ask, as I had to sell our business with little to offer. It was nerve-racking, and I was repeatedly rejected.

I decided to approach all the gyms, as I felt comfortable with my sporting background. After countless attempts, I began to make some progress and manoeuvred to set meetings with small gyms that were content only to place small orders, no more than 50 t-shirts. To me, any size order was a positive.

One day I took a deep breath and telephoned the Australia Institute of Sport (AIS) and talked my way up to the head buyer. I built a rapport with him over the phone in a short time. The quantities he was considering were huge, several thousand t-shirts, bags, caps and various other products. I was so excited as I was convinced I had struck it big. This would be the biggest sale in my career so far. After numerous discussions, the head buyer scheduled a trip to Sydney to discuss his requirements further. I was nervous and spent a lot of time ensuring that the room in Lina's house was set for the next day's meeting. I couldn't sleep a wink that night.

The following day, I arrived at Lina's early, anxious that all would be perfect for the two o'clock meeting. I waited and waited. Two o'clock came and went, with no sign of the client. Attempts to reach him by phone were unsuccessful. I was baffled and deeply disappointed. I racked my brain, trying to figure out what I'd done wrong, what could have happened. As I looked around, the realisation hit me. He had no doubt arrived at the house, realised this was a home-based business and decided there was no way a prominent outfit like the AIS was going to place such a huge order with some fly-by-night outfit. Looking back now I can laugh, but at the time it left me feeling profoundly disheartened. I knew I had to go on and focus on smaller clients who wouldn't baulk at our location.

Tough Times — Rudderless

My memories of this period are mainly of tough times. I felt rudderless. I had lost direction and lost touch with something I loved doing. I had no understanding of the merchandising industry. I'd gone from a comfortable corporate office to a room in a house in the suburbs, which I found demotivating. I recall my parents' deep concern, watching as I worked as hard as I could and barely earned a cent. That went on for about a year. Just working and working without any income to get the business on its feet. I was driving a beat-up old van; I had absolutely nothing. I'd rustle up $100 here and there, to help me survive but it was intensely frustrating to be unable to afford to buy so much as a drink if I went out with friends. I would order water or a beer to hold in my hand for hours so as not to feel conspicuous while mixing with the crowd.

Many of my friends advised me I was wasting my time. Why not get a proper job and earn an income, they asked. Part of me agreed with the sentiment, but another part told me to learn what I could to identify what other possibilities existed in the world. I told my well-meaning critics to wait and see where I would be in five years' time and then we could decide if I was truly wasting my time. I was determined to maintain a positive attitude, a belief in myself and my never-say-die passion to succeed.

I had many false starts before my star began to shine. There were many bumps and bruises on my road to success but through it all, yes, I stood tall and did it my way, never losing my drive and never losing my self-belief. Success speaks for itself. I had had enough of the negative comments ridiculing my intentions. Nothing or no one, I decided, was going to stop me from doing exactly what I had planned.

These thoughts were a catalyst, fuelling my drive even more. But in the interim, despite this belief, I found I couldn't ignore the call of the wild, or, in my case, the call to return to Lebanon (at this point, I should mention that I had already been to Lebanon twice before, both times touring with the Australian Lebanese basketball team. While I was there, one of the local team scouts had apparently spotted me).

A fax arrived from the president of the Rosaire Basketball Club asking to speak with me. I telephoned him and was stunned to learn he wanted me to try out for their team.

Basketball — Yet Again

My cousin's fledgling business didn't have many clients, so I decided she could manage well enough without me. I wanted to explore this once-in-a-lifetime opportunity to become a professional basketball player in the Middle East. Perhaps there was a hint of opportunism, but when Fate was dealing me such a card, I felt it would be foolhardy to ignore it.

Two days later, I was on a flight bound for Lebanon.

After a short trial with the team, they liked what they saw and offered me a player contract. After two more weeks, I flew back to Australia to organise a few final details and returned to Lebanon two months later. My parents were thrilled. Needless to say, it was the most exciting adventure I had ever had. I was ecstatic to have the chance to be the best I could be at my chosen sport and to play overseas. It is every person's dream to do what they love and be paid for it!

I arrived in Beirut in time for the pre-season camp. Playing in a foreign country was a real challenge. Admittedly, Lebanon was my place of birth, but I had lived all my life in Australia. Still, I was energised by the connection I felt.

Our training schedule was three times a day, six days a week. I lost the sense of passing time. I had days that felt like that movie, *Groundhog Day*. Day in, day out, our coach pushed us to our limits.

Whatever path you follow, whether it is a sport, business, or anything else, it comes with its unique set of challenges. Mental strength, along with emotional intelligence, plays a major part in how far you are prepared to go to be the best you can be.

Playing professionally overseas did come with its perks. I soon found myself on the front cover of sports magazines, on TV and being recognised for my profession. It was exhilarating. Amongst all the hype, it could have been easy to get derailed and lose focus on my goal.

Our first pre-season game took place in a small village against Sagesse, the Lebanese and Asian champions. I played for more than 30 minutes. I was guarding Elie Mchantaf who, at that time, was the best player in Lebanon. It was pretty daunting, but I managed to keep his scoring to a reasonable number.

A few months into my contract I began feeling the strain of internal club politics. The president had his favourite player another point guard and issues arose concerning me getting more court time than the other player did. The situation became so bad that I requested they release me so I could play with another team. I was frustrated. To make matters worse, they wouldn't release me until it suited them. The cut-off date for transfers was August 30. To my disgust, they waited until August 31 to release me to prevent me from playing with any other team. It was difficult not to feel bitter but, at age 23, I felt I had to accept that it just wasn't meant to be.

Deciding my goals and aspirations lay in the realm of the business world after all I turned my back on professional basketball for what I thought would be the final time. The umbilical cord had been severed, this time forever, I told myself. Nothing could have been further from the truth.

Back To Work

In the meantime, I flew back to Australia and focused on Lina's business, by which time George, Lina and Danny had joined forces. The combined business interests were getting traction and attracting more and more clients to the point where relocation to bigger premises became imperative. A better-defined structure emerged, and I found myself feeling comfortable in the corporate environment, enjoying a new sense of security and stability.

The business soon expanded and we secured several substantial accounts that yielded consistent cash flow to where we could afford to hire the additional staff we needed. The company continued to expand, and soon we found ourselves relocating yet again, to even bigger premises. My confidence was also growing as my understanding of the industry increased.

I turned my focus to gaining bigger and bigger clients. At this point I was managing numerous clients, each turning over just a few thousand dollars at a time. I looked at my production reports. I would have 80 jobs in production, with a total value of roughly $90,000. I needed to work smarter, I thought, not harder. I targeted the clients who had what I felt was the greatest potential and focused on them. This approach is referred to as the Pareto principle or 80-20 rule where roughly 80% of the yield comes from 20% of the sources. In my case, this meant focusing on the 20% of clients that offered the greatest dollar value return.

The following year I turned over $1.2 million in sales with considerably less effort. Despite the numbers, I was still the youngest of the four and knew I was last in everyone's minds. I felt somehow that I was going backwards instead of forwards. I had generated $1.2 million in sales but wasn't being given a chance to develop. The look in their eyes said, "We are more experienced, and we know more, so let us handle things." I, instead, was impatient, wanting to test my ability and push my boundaries.

It didn't help that I thought I was underpaid. Friends in the industry were being paid $60,000 to $80,000 for turning over $800,000 in sales. I, on the other hand, was turning over more than a million dollars in sales and getting $55,000 a year for my efforts. The disputes over salary were constant. I wanted to do right by the family, but at the time they wanted to hire and pay $45,000 apiece to two people to turn over $500,000 each in sales.

I said, "Wait a minute. Do the math. I'm turning over more than a million dollars in sales, and you want to pay these people $90,000 combined to do the same? Why shouldn't I be getting $90,000 then?" It seemed logical to me. However, this didn't go down well with George and Lina. Still, I was convinced I was right and was determined to stand up for myself.

On consideration I see that my observation of the way things were being run was the beginning, albeit subconsciously, of my formula. The need to keep things simple and effective.

As I looked around, I saw things that made me uncomfortable. It appeared to me that we spent a lot of money on things that did little or nothing for the infrastructure of the company. It seemed that my, as yet unformulated, mantra of spending wisely was not what was happening here.

And if the money wasn't being spent for the good of the company, how could the company be profitable?

Although the business had a healthy turnover, I thought it wasn't holding onto it.

I agree that money needs to be spent in order to grow but it is vital to keep the correct balance.

I mightn't have done things the way they were done, but in the long run I think it helped me a lot personally, because it reinforced my beliefs and thinking when I started my own company.

My disappointment grew as my passion for the business shrank. When my chance to become a sales manager was shot down, I knew I'd reached a turning point. I was told I was too young and had no real experience in management. I felt I had no choice, and so I resigned.

I told Danny I'd show him how to run a business properly. Danny told me it wasn't as easy as I thought and to stop being such a smartass.

I still lacked a vision for my first solo enterprise. In my quest for inspiration and direction, I decided on a radical approach. I left Australia.

So, began the next phase of my odyssey. It was the toughest, scariest thing I'd ever done. I left security behind to step into the unknown. And, let me tell you, that step out of my comfort zone was a giant, terrifying leap. There were dark moments when I was riddled with self-doubt. How could I be so stupid? So foolish? How could I walk out on my family business without knowing where I was going?

I squared my shoulders. If I had the willpower to take that first step, I reasoned, then I had the willpower to achieve something big. I didn't want to be a follower. I wanted to be a leader. I didn't want to be a dreamer. I wanted to be a doer.

I set off on what was intended to be a 10-week fact-finding trip to Europe. Ten weeks turned into six months as the vision of my future began to materialise.

Although I was enjoying the new experiences and new people like on any vacation, I also knew I was preparing for the next stage in my life to take flight. It was while I was in London that I experienced an epiphany of sorts and saw with great clarity what I wanted to do.

Entrepreneurial Strategies — Chapter Four

- Recognise and reward staff

- Don't blur the lines between business and friendship

- Tips for starting out

Recognise and reward staff

Good staff members are invaluable. If you want to hold on to your staff and build a strong, loyal culture within your business, consider implementing a reward scheme. The key to good management is to identify what drives your employees individually. Discover the stimulus that pushes them to strive for greatness. The reward need not be monetary. It could be a bonus day off to spend with their family or even an extra hour for lunch.

A points program where employees who achieve delineated goals earn points towards a free dinner, or a vacation is another possibility. One caveat: If you bribe your staff, there's a risk they will come to expect it as part of their normal compensation. I prefer to reward my people on a merit basis as it's often more appreciated.

If you thank a manufacturing group every time they make customer deliveries on time by providing them with a free lunch, gradually the lunch becomes a given, an entitlement, and is no longer viewed as a reward. For example, in one organisation, the CEO traditionally bought lunch for all employees every Friday. Soon, he had employees asking to be reimbursed if they ate lunch outside of the company on Fridays. His goal of team building turned into an entitlement with disappointing results.

Employee recognition is not just about doing something nice for people. Employee recognition is a communication tool that reinforces and rewards the most important outcomes people create for your business. When you recognise people effectively, you reinforce with your chosen means of recognition the actions and behaviours you most want to promote. When considering an employee recognition process, bear in mind you must develop recognition that is equally powerful for both the organisation and the employee.

Figuring out the most effective methods to reward and recognise employees is no simple task. The key thing is to express appreciation. A small thank you or acknowledgement has a positive impact.

Take the time to acknowledge and personally thank those employees who have improved production, efficiency and the overall mood of the office or job site.

Don't blur the lines between business and friendship

Finding the right balance between business and friendship boils down to respect. Often when small businesses start up, they naturally involve family and friends. After all, it is family and friends who support you through thick and thin and want you to succeed. But balancing the needs of personal and business relationships can be tricky if respect is not present. That means not giving — or expecting — special treatment when a personal relationship exists. This is equally important for those co-workers with whom you do not have a special relationship. It's imperative to treat everyone the same in business, no matter what the connection.

Set a tone of professional respect. All too often, managers confuse building camaraderie among employees with creating an overly familiar environment. When the work environment becomes too familiar, it is easy for employees to feel comfortable sniping and griping. And this is something you want to avoid at all costs!

Leadership involves motivating the entire staff to share a common vision. You can't effectively lead if you're trying to cultivate personal relationships instead of professional ones. If snipes and gripes begin to permeate your office culture, you must stop being a buddy and start being a leader. Direct your staff towards productive problem-solving sessions and activities to create the momentum to move forward.

Camaraderie, social activities, trust, and sincerity, are all important traits in a leader, but it is important to draw the line at becoming a friend to every team member. Being a leader is a very different role than being a friend or relative. You cannot be an objective leader, one who carries out the tough decisions and provides the necessary coaching/performance feedback to employees if you are also trying to be their friend or tiptoe around the implied debt of a family connection. Relationships have been damaged this way. Instead, cultivate a strong environment of trust and insist everyone keep things professional.

Tips for starting out

When I left the family business, I was wary of the unknown. My business grew quickly, but here are some tips that might have made that fear-filled stage easier.

Tip 1

Map out a plan. Make a to-do list, crunch the numbers and marshal your human and production resources. It is always easier to fight a battle in your head or on paper or computer spreadsheet than to shoot first and ask questions later. No matter how much pressure you're getting from your customers to deliver the goods right now, you need to take the time to sit down and map out a plan of attack. For a manufacturing company or a wholesale distributor, this means estimating how many units of product your customers might buy and how much it would cost to produce or import them. A service company like an ad agency or a web design firm must estimate how many additional employees or independent contractors are necessary to service the expected influx of new accounts.

If your company already has employees, ask if they're willing to put in a few extra hours to help you get over the hump. If you're a one-person show reach out to friends and family members to give you a temporary hand or if they lack the necessary skills, post ads on websites to find skilled freelancers and independent contractors. Be aware that your success may be temporary, so be prepared for peaks and troughs. Don't commit to hiring full-time employees with payroll taxes and benefits until you're sure your company's good fortune is secure.

Tip 2

Forge production partnerships. A small business making handcrafted soaps is going to be hard-pressed to fill a million-unit order from a large national chain all by itself. Partner with manufacturers who can take your samples or prototypes and reproduce them in large quantities. While there's no shortage of suppliers listed on the Internet a reliable manufacturer that delivers high-quality goods is not so easy to find. Your best bet may be to contact your industry's trade association and its leading trade publications (industry newspapers) for consultants and referrals.

Tip 3

Communicate with your customers. Communication is the lifeblood of any business relationship, but it is even more critical when your product or service suddenly takes off. The biggest mistake a business owner can make is failing to warn customers of shipping or production delays until it is too late.

Companies who fail to communicate with their key customers may find themselves not only with egg on their faces but with unsold inventory in their warehouses as well. There are so many things that are beyond your control. I would rather tell my customers the truth and have them be angry with me for five minutes than make excuses and burn my bridges forever.

Tip 4

Invest for the future. While it's tempting to reap the profits from your hit product right away, it is important to reinvest some of those profits to help your business grow. Whether this translates to paying down debt, buying new equipment, hiring employees or opening another location, don't pass up this opportunity to make your money work for you. It is always cheaper to put your own cash to work for you than to borrow money from a bank or relinquish equity to an investor.

Notes

Our young family on our arrival in Australia. My Father, Mother, older brother Danny and a very young me.

Early indicators of my character. Smiling optimism

My Under 16s team the Parramatta Wildcats. It was not only me (first left, bottom row) who went on to things beyond our early expectations, a young Justin Harrison (back row second left) later played rugby for the Australian Wallabies.

My 21st birthday, my brother Danny and my close friend Leon Trimmingham who had a very big impact on my life.

The road less travelled – where might I be now if I had pursued sport instead of business? Any ambitious athlete dreams of turning pro' and being paid to do what he loves! But I have no regrets.

My team, Rosaire Basketball club.
An experience I won't forget.

In Paris during my life-changing journey.

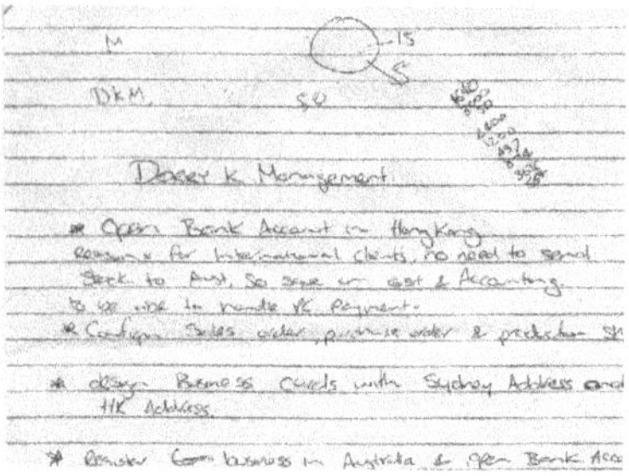

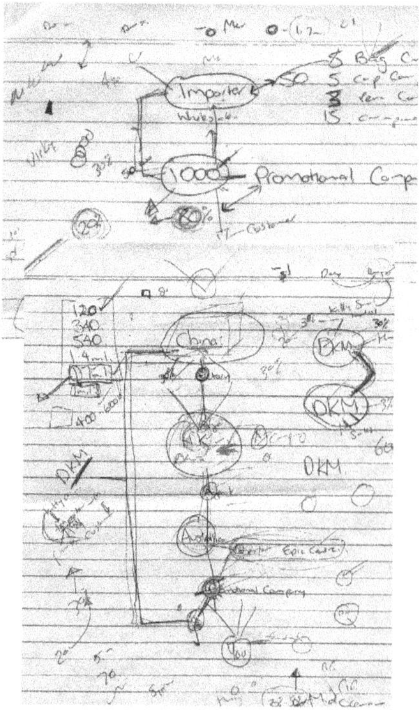

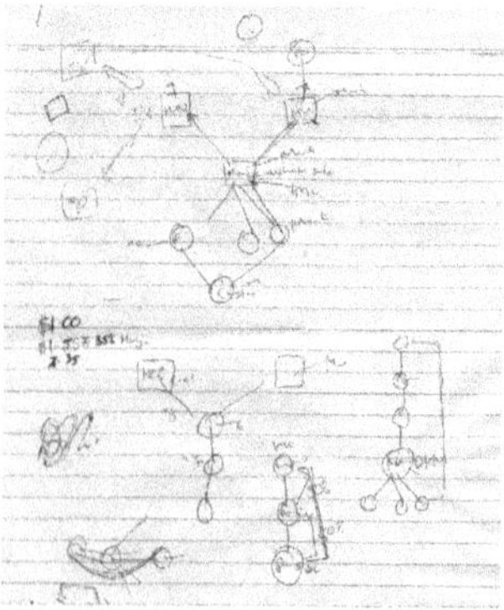

Many people told me I would need a beautifully presented multi-page business plan to succeed. Really? This is the basis of my Win Big Risk Small formula. I wrote it on during my 6-month European journey. And it worked!

Front covers of BRANDED, my vision realized!
With a circulation in excess of thirty thousand copies per issue, the magazine established really gave the company a competitive edge. It has also educated our customers and proven that good promotional merchandise can be the vehicle for valuable below the line advertising campaigns. Not just a series of cheap throwaways.

People who know me, know I like to socialize but I also believe it's a good form of business networking and have made numerous useful contact this way. Here I am with my brother David.

Celebrating, my nomination as a finalist with close friend Harry Cousens at the Ernst & Young Entrepreneur of the Year awards dinner.

It was also great for my family to celebrate my success. It validated their early faith in my ambitions.
Left to right: my sister Christine, mum, me and dad.

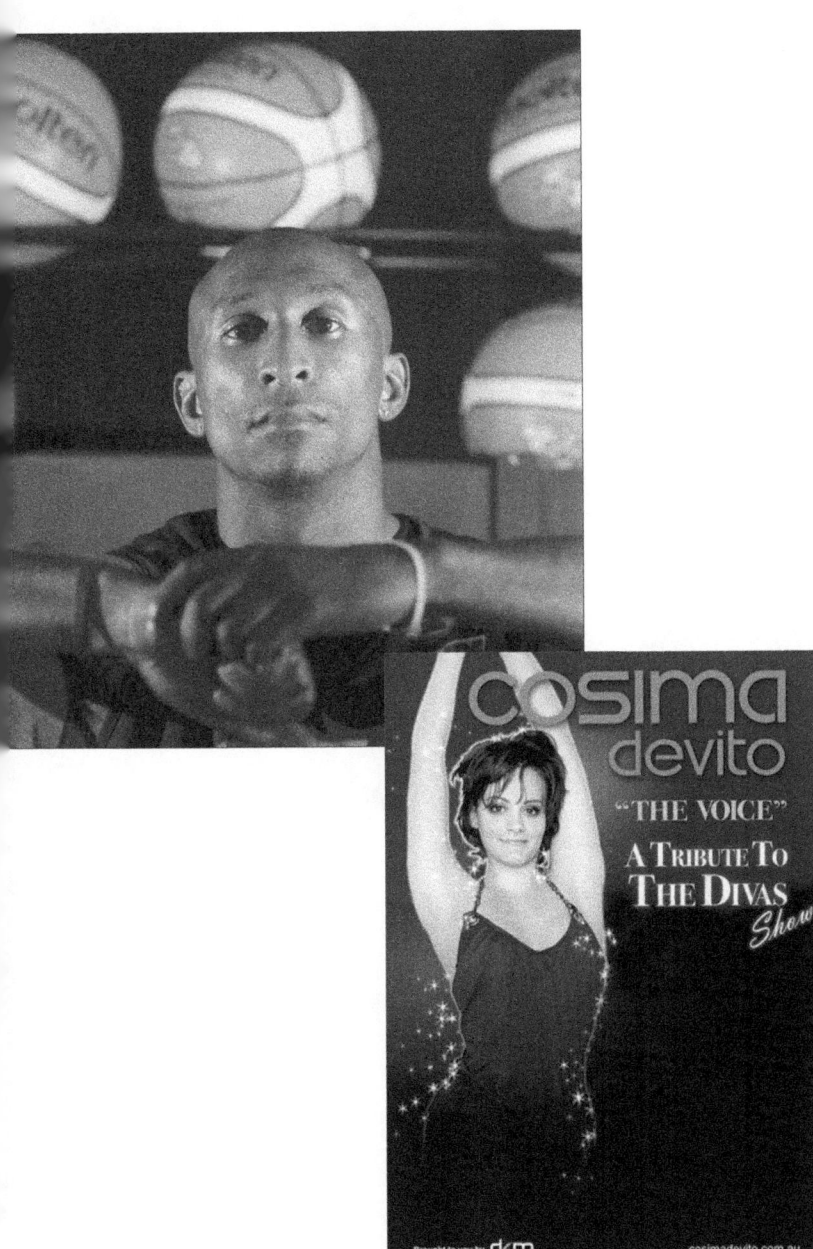

Pushing the Boundaries of my Comfort Zone!
Proving my abilities in highly diverse fields. Two of my early management signings.
Highly regarded US Import Kavossy Franklin
and
Cosima de Vito's poster from her appearance at the Sydney Opera House which was
the icing on the cake of my rebranding campaign for her

Chapter 5

Turning the Vision into Reality

I have always loved dealing, trading and negotiating. It has always been a part of who I am. When I was selling shoes, even at that young age, I would instinctively try to up-sell clients to two pairs of shoes instead of one, or guide the clients into a more expensive, better quality product.

The gift of the gab and an ability to relate to people helps a lot here. I've always been a good talker, and I have always loved helping people. So, for me, it was natural. I never went to university, never completed a TAFE course or obtained a marketing degree. It has all been about putting myself in the buyer's shoes (so to speak), and then listening to and perceiving what it is they want.

Being able to read another person is just as important as vision and just about as hard to teach. There is little doubt, however, that any successful businessperson possesses the ability to read the person sitting on the opposite side of the table. And not just to read them, but to visualise five steps ahead, like a chess player, instead of only one.

When I left Australia, I travelled throughout Europe, staying with anyone I knew to keep down costs. One of them was another cousin called George, who lived in Paris. He was heading south-east to Saint-Tropez for a holiday and suggested I accompany him. I knew nothing of Saint-Tropez, least of all that it was a playground for the rich and famous.

My cousin had hired a villa for a month at Sainte-Maxime, a nearby bay. From the moment I arrived, my eyes lit up, and I was overwhelmed by the lifestyle and the magnitude of the wealth I saw about me.

For ten days, it was non-stop partying at nightclubs until four or five o'clock in the morning, and then heading back to the villa for a quick nap, only to start all over again.

The first night I went to the V.I.P Room, which was reputed to be one of the best clubs. While there, I saw a sign for a Bad Boy party the following night, Bad Boy being the famous rapper, P. Diddy. It turned out to be a red carpet, invitation-only event. Celebrities were waltzing in; the paparazzi were out in force, and everyone was dressed to the nines. I watched as a car pulled up, and P. Diddy emerged.

I thought, "How the hell am I going to get into this party?" It took me half an hour to pluck up my courage, but I figured, "What the heck, I'm in another country, nobody here knows me."

My cousin was back at the villa and so if I got tossed out no one would find out. Taking a deep breath, I walked towards the entrance. There were 15 or so people ahead of me. To my amazement, the bouncer looked me up and down, parted the crowd and waved me through. I don't know who on earth he mistook me for, but I got in.

Inside, guests were outdoing each other, buying the most expensive Champagnes. Meanwhile, I stood holding my solitary beer, which had cost a shocking price, taking tiny sips and trying to make it last all night. I saw a world I had never seen before or even realised existed. If anything, this made me even hungrier for the extreme success I knew could be mine if I strove hard enough.

The next day I linked up with the same glitterati on Nikki Beach where the festivities continued. With strains of "if my friends could see me now," strumming through my brain, I returned to the V.I.P Room. Twenty metres from the entrance, the bouncer spotted me. By the time I had reached the door, he had parted the crowd to permit me to pass. To this day, I suspect he had confused me with someone else, but back then I wasn't about to ask. What I did discover was that wealth and success brought privilege and status and I wanted it — more than ever!

After finagling my way into other purportedly impenetrable V.I.P nightspots across Europe, I started to ask myself some penetrating questions. If I were to start a company and sell products from the modest back garden of my parents' home, how would I convince people to buy from me? Would I need to lower my margins and undercut all the competition? Or should I make my company look like a million dollars and focus on branding and brand placement? With my new penchant for the finer things, quality and luxury, I chose the latter. This wasn't solely based on a purely hedonistic attitude but rather on the observation that most of my prospective competitors in the marketplace were just going through the motions of moving product.

Is Promotion The Key?

My perspective was shaped by my European experience, where I witnessed first-hand the significant differences between the promotions industry in Australia versus overseas. Europe is very image conscious. Everything is so well done. They have so much style. You don't see the usual gear; everything is carefully thought out. I began to wonder why Australians didn't take the same degree of care with their image as Europeans did with theirs.

In Australia, armed with a bag of goodies and a catalogue, the competition almost exclusively relied on customers to sell to themselves. If I was to make my company look like a million dollars, I needed to differentiate myself from the competition. I didn't need a degree to open a promotional business, but I knew I would need a philosophy of branding, brand platforms, high-quality work and, equally as important, the ability to manage clients' needs and expectations instead of just telling them what they should need. In other words, I was going to turn the traditional promotional methods upside down. I would position myself as an assistant to my clients, an indispensable right arm they could trust and rely upon without question. After all, the more a person trusts, the less they question. In other words, the more they feel comfortable with how you do business, the less likely the client is to shop around for alternatives. This has been my philosophy from day one, and it works.

Making the Client's Job Easier

My business has continued to grow and improve because I view it from a management perspective, not a product perspective. To me, the product is secondary. Sure, I can put a logo on a cap or print it onto a t-shirt, but what sets my firm apart is how we approach making the client's job easier, saving them time which, in turn, increases their reliance upon us. The smart clients are not going to give their business away to someone else to save 10 cents if they are spending 30% more time to save that extra 10 cents.

European Excellence

I began with the vision that the merchandising industry should be mainly about managing clients' expectations. I didn't want to be a provider of merchandise. I looked at it from the perspective that I would manage their business by becoming part of their marketing team. If they didn't have a marketing team, well, then I was going to be their marketing manager, marketing assistant or brand manager. With that strategy, I would elevate my business beyond needing to compete with my so-called competitors. I created a niche market where, instead of competing on price, I competed on concepts and ideas. It took me six months to plan my strategy, which gave me both the time and the materials to surmount any fears of failure I experienced.

I spent many days in London walking the streets for hours and hours, assessing all the positives and negatives. I spent months visualising the possible potholes in the business strategy and how I would overcome them. I changed my return flight six times, determined not to return until I was as fully prepared as possible and had a clear direction of the way I was going to build my business — my empire. I had no intention of starting my own business until those thoughts were straight in my mind. Once I had it all worked out, I flew home the very next day and began.

When I returned from Europe, my family probably thought I'd walk in with my tail between my legs, begging to return to the family business. It would have been reasonable to assume that a holiday would calm my state of mind. But I came back fired up, ready to challenge myself, affirmed in my belief that there was no room whatsoever for failure. I certainly didn't intend to return to cutting people's hair for the rest of my life, and I had even less intention of crawling back to the family business. Somewhere, somehow, I was determined to find the answers, to make it on my own.

I hate losing. I'm extremely competitive. I'm a fighter, and whether it may be called pride or determination, nothing was going to beat me down. Taking that first step into the unknown is probably one of the hardest steps any person will ever take but taking it is what sets you apart, as someone who takes action, not someone who is going to hold back because of either fear, disbelief or both. I had already decided before I left Europe that I could not return to Australia until everything was clear in my head.

I am sometimes asked about what difficult times I've had in business and I can't say I've had too many. I think this is due to my mental approach prior to setting up the business of working through all the potential potholes before I'd even started.

Push Yourself Beyond Boundaries

I committed to constantly pushing myself beyond the boundaries of my comfort zone. Having already faced the biggest challenge of leaving the family business to go it alone in the wilderness, without any formal education behind me, I knew I had no room for failure. That was not a place I was prepared to go. All I had to start this empire was a desk, a computer and a whole heap of attitude. I built a website, printed up some business cards and the adventure began. I managed all aspects of the business. I was the sales manager, the accountant, the production manager and the logistics manager. I made sure I knew every part of my business before I contemplated hiring anyone. It was important to me to gain experience in all aspects of my business and doing so allowed me to understand the roles my future staff members would play. I kept it simple and used spreadsheets for invoicing. I created a numeric tracking system for my orders. My parents' backyard became a warehouse. I would receive stock from China and have to hold over 100 boxes at a time. It was like a makeshift external warehouse where I would run my logistics by doing the labelling and dispatching myself. Back then my entire marketing pack was printed on a single piece of A4 paper.

When I first started, a lot of suppliers failed to support me the way I needed because they saw me as a small-time, backyard operator. The few who did support me are among those I use today. I have been loyal to those who have helped me build my business, in appreciation for their loyalty. We continue to grow our commercial relationships, and for that, I am very thankful. The positive side of this relationship is that it affords me negotiating power with my suppliers, allowing me to remain competitive in the market. The lesson learnt here is that building a strong supplier relationship is a critical part of one's business. They have seen my business grow to the success it is today, and they have been rewarded with gaining my business. Today we have a lot of suppliers knocking on our door wanting to offer their services. I stay true to those who looked after me when I ran my logistics from the backyard of my parents' home.

Keep in mind that, before you start placing orders overseas, you must calculate how much working capital you will need to meet the market demand. Though not unheard of, it is unlikely that you can negotiate terms with your supplier to be paid after you get paid. Also, as you will need to pay your employees and general overheads during the same period, you'll require a source of capital that you can tap into immediately.

Gain Respect

One hurdle I faced was being respected as a business leader. I always had a bit of a complex about being seen as too young. I feared people wouldn't take me seriously when it came to business. I had experienced this as part of the family business and didn't want the same thing to happen within my own business. When I started DKM at the age of 25, I was driven to succeed and to show everyone not to judge me by my age but by my success and work ethic. Maybe I worried too much about it as, for a short time, I was filled with self-doubt. However, in hindsight, it also served to give me the desire to work harder than the next person and push myself to heights I never previously thought I could achieve. Pretty soon I stopped worrying about the age factor.

Just as Richard Branson had done, I created the impression to the outside world that I was running a sizeable and established business, when, in fact, I was working from inside a garden shed. Even if a prospective customer hadn't heard of me, I managed to convince them to give me a try and, if I couldn't deliver, then I didn't expect them to buy from me. So, as a fledgling entrepreneur, I was ready to test my wings and to see if they would allow me to soar to great heights or plummet to my doom before I could figure out how to make them flap.

The first thing that I had done when I returned from Europe was to register DKM (Dorry Kordahi Management) as a company, and from that point, I have never looked back. Within six months, this fledgling entrepreneur had taken his first faltering flight into the world of the business tycoon. And though I wasn't making much money, I was acquiring a sound client base with my unique approach to branding from Day One.

I even inspired my older brother, Danny. Upon seeing how quickly I was establishing myself, he thought, *if he can do it, so can I!* So, Danny then left the family business and registered his company under the name DK Blue.

Your First Employee

All too soon it was time to think about hiring my first employee. First, I elicited some assistance from my good friend, Elisa Grant, whom I first met at an industry event, the Australian Promotional Products Association's (APPA) Christmas function back when I was still working for Lina, my cousin. Elisa and I became friends, and she spent a lot of time with me, brainstorming ways in which I could succeed in my own business.

Working only a suburb away from each other, I would meet Elisa for lunch regularly. We would bounce ideas off each other and talk about the industry, exploring ways in which we could maximise our business opportunities. She also furnished me with leads when she knew she couldn't satisfy the client through her organisation.

Now that I needed to hire someone, I knew Elisa could help. Elisa had been a recruitment consultant before coming into the industry, so we had very different backgrounds. Hers was strong in direct sales because, in recruitment, you are essentially selling thin air; it is quite different from selling tangible products. She'd also been to university and completed several sales courses. As a result of our numerous conversations, I began to view certain aspects of my planning in a different light. This experience was very beneficial. It was a strong combination of skills, education, and experience that we brought to the table. We would endlessly discuss suppliers and supply channels, and I would quiz her on how a person could sell if they didn't know what they were selling (i.e. recruitment). She explained how it didn't matter what you were selling, that sales principles are consistent no matter what the product or service.

Even though she'd only been in the brand merchandising business about six months when we met, she had already won some significant accounts. I knew I could sell but I was hungry to learn how she achieved her results and, in return, I offered her the benefit of my years of industry knowledge.

I discussed my need to hire someone with Elisa. It took about six months before it came to fruition and by that time she had begun working for Corporate Express.

Her new company was one of the major players in our industry. I remember her asking me how I imagined I could compete with such a giant organisation and I replied, "Believe me, I'll compete!" My reasoning was that the bigger you are, the harder it is to manoeuvre, which turned out to be true as Corporate Express is no longer in operation. I explained I'd rather be a swift cheetah able to dart in a different direction with deft ease when chasing its prey, than a lumbering elephant that had only its size to rely on.

She laughed, but during that six-month period when she came to my office in the back garden, I continued to pepper her with questions and get her to help without ever actually employing her.

The first employee I hired was my younger brother, David. At the time, David had been working in retail for many years with no clear direction. He came to me and asked if I could give him an opportunity in a new field. I insisted he was formally interviewed before I made my decision. I asked Elisa if she would assist with the interviewing process. She was surprised, but my reasoning was sound. I had already learned from having operated a family business that sharing the same blood does not equate to working well together. Elisa was experienced both in my chosen industry and in recruitment, so even though I might be putting her in a bit of a spot, I knew she would make an unbiased and informed assessment as to whether or not I should hire David.

Elisa suggested we conduct the interview in a local pub. Although the atmosphere was relaxed and casual, the conversation was extremely serious and pointed.

After the interview had concluded, Elisa and David shared a few glasses of wine and a laugh. At this time, Elisa advised David that this was, in fact, a serious business he would be joining, that it was going places and how his brother wasn't going to employ him simply because he was family. He was going to have to earn his position like any other candidate.

As it turned out, our first attempt at working together may not have felt like a match made in heaven, but now our working relationship is a solid one.

Back in the days of working in the garden shed, part of the problem arose with mindset. It might have looked like a garden shed, smelled like a garden shed and been situated in a position where you might expect to find a garden shed, but, to me, this was my first official premises, and I expected it to be treated as such. I would dress professionally to go to work. I would go out for my lunch. In every aspect, I treated this garden shed like my corporate office. David, on the other hand, treated it like a garden shed. He wore whatever he felt like and took a nap inside at lunchtime. Annoyed, I asked him if he'd do that in an office. Of course not, he said, but this wasn't an office, he pointed out. It was a garden shed. And therein lay the difference in attitude between us. It required a mental willingness, a discipline to treat the business as a business, no matter what the physical location was. Regrettably, after several months, I felt I had no option but to fire David because he stubbornly refused to share the DKM philosophy. I suggested he work with our older brother, Danny, so that he would have to commute to work and understand and appreciate the importance of discipline.

Although I often light-heartedly suggested Elisa become an employee of DKM, I now became unrelenting in my pursuit of her. I would frequently speak at length to her about leaving her high-flying, secure, corporate position to risk it all and join my fledgling empire. Finally, I wore her down.

The first three months were tough on Elisa. She thumbed through the Yellow Pages making cold calls to businesses, as I had once previously done in my cousin's apartment. She was in conflict with my philosophies, largely because I wasn't doing things the way they had been done at Corporate Express. I was resolute in my beliefs; it was my way or not at all. Elisa came not only to respect my business nous but also over time evolved into one of my biggest advocates.

In an uncharacteristic but mercifully brief period of waning confidence, I grew afraid to expand my business. In my first few years of operation, my annual turnover had reached one million dollars and I, understandably I now believe, suddenly decided this was comfortable. I didn't want to spend what I saw as an extortionate amount on rent. After all, I was turning over a million dollars a year without an office. The bottom line was that I had let fear seep into my consciousness. I had already taken that first terrifying step that some never do by going out on my own.

Now I was presented with another challenge — taking the next step. Would we remain forever at a million-dollar turnover working out of a garden shed? Certainly, I could do worse and certainly this limited my exposure to risk. But I wanted to acknowledge that what my parents had seen in me when they first let me set up in their backyard was something more?

I wanted to prove to them that their faith had been justified. That I could grow my company and become a success. Besides, did I really want to stay in a backyard?

That, of course, was a rhetorical question but to move to the next level, to face that risk head on, to continue challenging myself as I'd always told myself I wanted to do, required me to stick my neck out into unfamiliar territory once again. So, I prepared myself mentally and pushed myself out of my comfort zone and into what I hoped was a new tomorrow, pushing my boundary of fear to a new level. Ultimately, the next level became my next comfort zone and, hence, to continue expanding, this entire exercise had to be repeated.

I focused on streamlining the business to the point where I could withstand any turbulence. I built up my cash reserve to a point where, if I didn't have another sale for three years I would still be able to support the business with its current overhead. My aim was to have a secure business where I could dictate to the market, not have the market dictate to me. When companies start making money, they often overcapitalise or take on unnecessary costs because they either think they need it or they want to impress. A business is measured on profit, not on its turnover.

In an industry with over 2,000 competitors, I realised I would need to bring something different to the table to gain market share rapidly enough. I think it is important to elaborate the difficult industry that I am in. I am not in a retail space or an industry that has huge potential to make large amounts of money. Margins are low and competition fierce. A tendency to bring down the market costs on price wars can naturally hurt the industry, not only from a price perspective but also from the point of view that products and services might be devalued in the eyes of marketing and brand managers alike. Remember the focus of where I positioned my business? Not just as someone coordinating logos on tangible goods. I was here to create an impact by being the service provider this industry had never experienced before. I managed to make my money in a tough industry, which turned out to be very rewarding and gave me the reassurance that I was running my business in the direction of growth and prosperity, not just survival.

Elisa was my right-hand person for a good part of the developmental stage. I had the major accounts, but Elisa did a lot of the administration, such as compiling the job specifications, creating systems and procedures, as well as forms and everything else a business needs to grow. She confessed there were periods where she felt it was all too much and she wasn't getting what she needed out of the position. She obviously wanted this to work for both of us, though, because she stuck it out. That decision ultimately paid dividends, but it wasn't always that way.

For a long time, Elisa received anything but preferential treatment, and that was one of the reasons she would get upset. She would ask why I would get angry with her. She didn't understand initially that she needed to be perceived as leading by example. Even though we were friends, it was still a business relationship we were in and that had to be made abundantly clear to everyone around us. After all, I had adopted the same policy with my younger brother David and I felt this situation could be no different. Often, she had to prove herself more in some instances, and that was something that did cause her some angst.

Criticisms are sometimes levelled at me for being a little too self-assured. I find that laughable because, in business, if you can't come across as supremely confident in what you do and who you are, then you are not going to instil confidence in anyone else. It is a necessary quality in this dog-eat-dog world. You need to set yourself head and shoulders above the crowd if you're going to be noticed and indeed if you are going to be taken seriously.

If you wish to emulate my success, you need to portray confidence and success and believe in yourself but at the same time remember who you really are. Do not forget who helped you get there because as I have said before 'no man is an island.' There will always be those you will need to recognise, reward and appreciate along the way.

At the same time, never let the lines blur between business and friendship or indeed business and family. Don't allow people to take advantage of you by making you feel guilty or convince you that you owe them something. Maintain sight of who your friends are and how to maintain those friendships. If these are people who genuinely care about you, they will support you on your journey.

Entrepreneurial Strategies — Chapter Five

- Taking risks sets you apart from the crowd

- Portraying confidence will give you confidence

- Never give up

Taking risks sets you apart from the crowd

Every entrepreneur takes risks. You're not going to be successful if you don't but it is important to stipulate that these should be calculated risks. Don't gamble.

Every risk I've taken has been a calculated risk. It hasn't been a risk that is going to jeopardise my business. The lesson is this: when you spend, spend wisely and only spend up to a point where you're not exposing yourself.

Taking a big risk is a gamble, but to me, it is more important to understand how to risk a little to gain a lot.

A successful entrepreneur knows the difference between the right and the wrong opportunity. You are always going to have opportunities in life, but you need to identify the right ones to pursue. Don't make the mistake of thinking that, if you don't take up an opportunity, you are going to miss out on getting in the game. Opportunities always arise, and the smart entrepreneur is the one who chooses the right opportunity. So, know your limitations. If the risk is so steep it can potentially damage your business, then that is an opportunity you need to forego.

The keys to managing risk are:

- Recognising why you may fear a certain decision or action and assessing if there is any rational justification for it.

- Knowing that many of the risks you avoid will reappear in the future.

- Understanding that growth and success come with risk and knowing that while you have everything to gain, you could lose everything if your risk becomes a gamble. Remember, risking more than you can afford to lose is no longer a risk, it's a gamble.

- Realising that risk is not about what other people do, think, feel or believe about your actions or decisions.

Portraying confidence will give you confidence

In business and life, you must portray confidence. Without confidence, people aren't going to want to do business with you. When you are trying to sell a product, if you don't believe in your product, how are you going to sell it? You've got to convey that belief in your product. I always say to my staff, if you don't enjoy what you're doing, don't do it, because it's going to show. You need to come across as if you know what you're talking about. So, learn everything you need to know as confidence can only go so far if it has no substance.

You don't have to ascribe to his politics but just watch someone like Canada's Justin Trudeau if you want some free master classes.

A large part of what has made me who am began with building relationships and networking and though social media is now a big part of my life, I don't think it's all of it. I am not saying that modern communication channels are not important, they are. But, in my opinion, as humans we should use these things to complement our overall social interaction skills, not replace them.

What is really important about self-confidence is it gives you the ability to read the signs of any meeting, whether it is in business or life and learn about other people and gauge their perception of you.

Learning to use eye contact and read people's reactions by their body-language is a very important part of this and obviously can only be done face to face. Put bluntly, using a dating app might allow you to meet someone but it can't make them like you.

The rise of social media has brought us into contact with the entire word and many people's pursuit of the perfection they are exposed to has led to an explosion of almost pandemic levels of low self-esteem and a lot of unhappiness.

It is a perfect example of people focussing on landing on a mountain, not climbing it and it doesn't have to be like that.

Half the battle is in your mind and the one thing you must never lose control of is your free will to determine how you react to any given situation. You can do something about how you portray your confidence to the world, so the only question that remains is: will you?

Never give up

If you have a dream and you believe with a passion that what you're doing is right, you must keep telling yourself to get up one more time, every time you are knocked down. You must never forget that each time someone tells you that you can't do something, each time someone says what you're doing doesn't have any market value, each time you hear this negative you have moved one step further along the path to finding the person that will say yes. They're out there; whether they are your first client, your first publisher, your first business partner or whoever else it may be. Keep searching, and you will find them.

Notes

Chapter 6

The Fledgling

As I said, my business expanded to the point where I was able to start looking for my first official premises. My first office was in Stanmore and cost $35,000 a year in rent, which was a little daunting after not having paid any rent previously. I was a bit apprehensive about making such a big financial commitment at the time, but it had to be done; it was all part of the plan and all part of the necessary requirements for growth and expansion. Before long, I also took over the office next door, doubling my floor space and remained there for the next five years. At that point in my journey, the company consisted of me, Elisa and three other staff members. One of the next lessons I learned along the way came during this phase — patience.

Managing staff wasn't an issue; however, trying to instil my philosophies into new staff members was another matter entirely, especially when dealing with a group of people whose beliefs and drives were at differing levels. In the early stages, I couldn't understand why everyone just didn't see things the way I did. For me, it was so obvious it should have been natural. Nonetheless, as I've pointed out before, if everyone thought the same way and achieved at the same level there would be no room in this world for achievers to rise to the top. While this may be self-evident, I was not the most patient man in the world; in fact, I was completely the opposite. When I wanted something, I wanted it right then. There were only two time-frames in my world — now and straightaway!

When you run a business, you need to learn patience and to be calm because not every staff member will possess the same degree of drive and ambition to succeed like you. I had to accept that many people, whether by disposition or circumstance simply want or need a job. If answering the phone all day paid them enough for their expenses and they were content, that was enough for them. As a driven person, it took me some time to understand and accept people for what they were.

Being driven is all well and good, but I have come to recognise, impatience is a flaw that must be overcome. All my staff members, apart from Elisa, were young and raw and for a good reason. Even if some of my young personnel were less driven than I, they had not yet fallen into immovable traits that might not fit within my business model and philosophy. The young and untrained are the most receptive to being trained and moulded, not to mention they also command lower salaries. I'd rather build experience than buy it.

Within three months of working for DKM, I had my staff producing the desired results for the most part, which was a win-win situation for everyone. The staff were learning valuable lessons and techniques, and I had them performing according to my standards without the need to pay senior rates. They, in turn, were making themselves more valuable in the market. In time, they would achieve better results and salaries as a consequence of my training.

With my tight-knit team, I soon reached a turnover of $3 to 4 million per year, in an industry that typically required 15 to 20 staff members to achieve the same result. This is another important lesson to learn: keep it simple. If you follow this business model, you can achieve good results with a smaller payroll and thus become more profitable. The bottom line is in the profit and loss statement, not what your staff complement looks like. I was able to achieve this result with minimal staff by teaching them how to multi-task, which in turn added further to their value and marketability. My staff learned new and valuable skill sets beyond the limits of their job description.

Right from the beginning, DKM had an interest in China. As most of us know, if you can successfully operate a business with a Chinese connection, if you get that part of your operation established, there is good money to be made because you can import directly. As a direct importer, your margins will be much greater and, in the case of DKM, Shanghai was a part of the operation from Day One via a Chinese colleague with whom I had established a relationship.

I'd discovered the type of margins that could be made quite by accident back when I was working at Lina's company. One of our suppliers at that time sent me an email. About two minutes later he called, panicked and cried, "Delete the email. It's a virus. Delete the email. It's a virus."

I said, "Don't worry, I'll delete the email." However, I didn't delete the email. My curiosity got the better of me. I know now I took a real risk when I opened the attached spreadsheet. Fortunately, it was not a virus. Instead, it contained their buying costs from a supplier in China.

I saw immediately they were making great margins. That was my first exposure to the possibilities that lay in doing business with China. It was my good luck to see that information, but it was knowing how to use it to my advantage that has been one of the keys to my business success. That's when I started delving into China.

There is a contemporary anecdote to add here that illustrates the synchronicity that has sometimes, beneficially, occurred in my career. Though that email came from a local supplier, those buying costs were

Chapter 6 The Fledgling

from one of the largest promotional and premiums suppliers in Europe.

And I never imagined back in the days when I first started DKM in my parents' garden shed, that I would one day be in a joint venture with them. And yet, just a couple of years ago, that's exactly what happened. I now have an exclusive distribution agreement with that very same European company which further cements DKM Blue's position as pre-eminent in its market.

Back then, I realised that if I got the China element correct it would make my business far more profitable than a standard promotional business. With over 2,000 competitors, I needed a key advantage. With that in mind, I flew to China to meet the agents and met a young kid, Jimmy, who was very new and inexperienced. I admired his passion to understand the business better. Consequently, when I arrived back in Australia, I spent a lot of time with him online teaching him everything I could. He spoke English fairly well, which was a massive asset; in fact, it would later prove vital. I explained to him about products, the industry and what Australia is like because he had never been outside China.

I would come home late each night, head out to the garden shed, go online and we would cyber-chat for two to three hours. Eventually, I suggested he leave his employer and set up his own company in China. He saw the opportunity I could bring him in the Australian market. I would concentrate on feeding him sales and he could focus solely on the supply aspect. It was a perfect fit.

Over the years, his company has grown alongside mine and we remain strong allies to this day.

I flew Jimmy to Australia and spent time educating him about the values of the Australian market, the quality of products, and what was and was not acceptable. As a result, he developed a clear and in-depth understanding of my expectations and standards, of the driving forces and market needs of DKM.

Jimmy started out as a one-man operation in China and now has a dozen staff members. It gives me pleasure to see how successful Jimmy has become. It is in part a result of our relationship that DKM is such a profitable operation.

As DKM merchandise is imported directly, it bypasses the middleman and minimises costs. No middleman also means faster, more responsive service across its range of more than 12,000 promotional items.

It also didn't hurt to have Shanghai as one of the locations listed on the letterhead, emulating once again one of Richard Branson's techniques for success in making your operation look bigger than it is without being dishonest.

I had always thought it would be great for DKM to have an interstate presence. I knew I had a business

Chapter 6   The Fledgling

trip coming up in Melbourne, so I started researching property prices on the internet.

I found one property I thought would be worthwhile checking out. It was an office on St Kilda Road, one of the main hubs of business in Melbourne, priced at $240,000. I called the agent for an appointment to inspect it.

I knew that the property had been on the market for a year, so I figured I would offer something ridiculous to see if the buyer would bite. After reviewing the suite, I made an offer of just over half the asking price, $130,000. I said to the agent that if the owner agreed, I would confirm the purchase there and then. The agent laughed. There was no way, he said, the owner would go that low. I suggested the agent call the owner anyway, assuring him I was prepared to write a cheque for the full amount there and then.

At the time there were numerous suites that were vacant in the building, so I believed the ball was in my court. I suspected that if the owner proved desperate, he would consider any offer on the table. I overheard the agent in the hallway as he spoke to the owner. To the agent's surprise and my delight, the owner accepted the offer.

Such is my luck, or perhaps the lesson here is the value of chutzpah. In other words, if you don't ask the question, how will you give someone the opportunity to accept? OK, they could refuse but then you'd be no worse off than you were before you asked. In a nutshell, that is how Melbourne came to be added to the locations of DKM.

From that point, the DKM letterhead legitimately reflected locations in Sydney, Melbourne, and Shanghai. It looked quite impressive for a total staff complement of five.

I pooled all my energy into building my brand. This effort was rewarded when, in 2005, the DKM logo was named by the international logo ratings agency Logo Lounge as one of the world's most exceptional logos. DKM was on stage next to brands like Microsoft, GE, Intel, and Bentley!

Logo Lounge has a booklet produced in New York every five years. My old friend and graphic designer, Corey Gross, who was familiar with the publication, said it was something to which all designers aspire. Together we played around with a few ideas to submit for consideration, finally agreeing on a design that was then selected as among the top 2,000 in the world. Having one of the world's most exceptional logos may not appear to mean much, but when your entire business is based on managing other people's images and profiles, it is vital to have some credentials on the board for your own image management before you can speak with credibility to others about managing theirs. That's when I came up with the slogan, "If we couldn't look after our own brand, how do you expect us to look after yours?"

Brand integrity is what we do. We can't say we are the market leaders and not take care of our own brand.

Of course, I understand that it isn't just about winning awards. You could come up with the slickest logo design ever created, but if the product behind it doesn't stack up, then you're not going to be able to take on the competition and gain greater market share.

Let's look at the Samsung debacle. In 2016 they held the number one spot on international listings for the smartphone sector with about 30% market share. Yet in that same year their latest model was launched as a worldwide disaster when the company was forced to recall 2.5 million units because they were fire hazards. In just six months it is estimated that the cost to Samsung was US$5.3 billion dollars. And yet, it goes much deeper than immediate dollar cost alone. The negative impact on brand Samsung had a lasting, negative effect which some analysts estimated put the full year cost closer to US$17 billion. For a company valued at the time at around US$300 billion and massive cash reserves, this amount is almost trivial, but the fact that pundits dropped their world ranking position from 1 to 11 in the space of a year is infinitely more serious. Remember what happened to Nokia in my Case Studies? Brand credibility is crucial.

I have found now that marketing managers are becoming more astute and starting to realise that they can drive their dollar further by using 'below-the-line marketing,' which is also referred to as 'merchandising.' I identified this as an issue ahead of the pack and incorporated it into my philosophy from the first in my new business. Part of this philosophy crystallised while

I was in Europe trying to consolidate my action plan to set myself apart from the competition. I set out to change the mentality of my industry and to that end began penning articles espousing my philosophy within trade magazines. Through perseverance and belief, DKM was soon seen as a business of substance with exceptional standards and excellence in client service that my competitors in the market now have to match. Mine has become the benchmark in the industry.

Like Richard Branson in the airline industry, the vision that broke the mould has made me a market leader. Many people fantasise about leading the lifestyle of any of these market leaders, but the reality is there are few with vision and even fewer prepared to put themselves out there and take the necessary risks. Success in any field of endeavour has never been achieved without taking risks. Climb to the peak of a mountain, and there is generally a high-velocity wind from those who covet your position ready to blow you off.

Entrepreneurial Strategies — Chapter Six

- Establish and build relationships with the best allies

- Hire young staff and train them in your image

- Keep it simple and don't overstaff

- Make your operation look as big as possible, without lying about it

- Compete for awards

Establish and build relationships with the best allies

Anyone and everyone who can help you achieve your objectives is a potential ally. Some are natural allies. For example, the people who share a common interest with you — the colleague who has been around for years and can offer an invaluable voice of experience, the team member who is always happy to be a sounding board for your ideas, or the vendor who is ready to accept seemingly impossible deadlines — these people are your natural allies. You can find allies in unexpected places too. Consider Arthur in finance, who pulls together an extra report on your project's finances; Sandy, the secretary, who tells you when the boss is in a good mood; or Fred, ex Head of Department who is always available for advice — they are all important allies.

This is why it is imperative to be open and supportive to others in the workplace and why it is worth making an effort to help others out when they need it. If you're a positive and supportive person, most people will be equally supportive of you.

With more formalised alliances between businesses, there are some personal qualities that a business owner and alliance partner, like a supplier, should ideally possess:

- Vision: It is a bad idea to develop an alliance just because it seems to be the right thing to do or is in line with existing trends. It is essential to develop a mutually beneficial vision, along with the ability to look at the future prospects and not become too dependent upon your alliance partner. You need to develop the vision to work towards creating successful alliances that benefit both parties.

- Curiosity: Keep looking for new opportunities to raise profits and improve your capabilities. It pays to be open to new and unexpected opportunities and to be curious about alliance possibilities.

- Communication: Lack of communication can lead to the failure of an alliance. Every business owner should focus on transparency and effective communication.

- Organisation: Organising the alliance structure and procedures can have a huge impact on the longevity and ultimate implementation of the alliance. If the adopted alliance structure is complex, keep all details and documents organised. This helps to develop a long-lasting and profitable alliance.

- **Leadership:** Develop leadership that highlights your willingness to focus on getting things done, rather than an obsession with being right all the time. This will affect and determine the success of your alliance. This attitude should be present at the very start of your business.

- **Compassion:** Compassion, along with tolerance, should be maintained in an alliance. These qualities help you to handle difficult situations and maintain your sanity.

- **Contracts:** Written agreements are vital to the success of an alliance, no matter how loyal and trusting each alliance partner is. Your expectations of one another and the promises you make should be documented and available for viewing whenever required.

Alliance relationships can be extremely profitable for all the parties involved. If you are confident and aware of all the steps involved, you will be well on your way. Of course, that is but one form of alliance. Alliances useful to your business will come in many shapes and sizes.

"A problem shared is a problem halved," as the old saying goes and it is true in business as well. When working your way through the challenges you face every day, it is a great help to be able to draw on a network of supportive individuals to find solutions. Allies are the people who give you backing, assistance, advice, information, protection and even friendship. They comprise your support base. With strong, mutually beneficial relationships with your allies, you can survive and thrive in the corporate arena, enabling you to get things done more quickly and smoothly. Working together with allies helps you and they achieve more than if you worked independently.

Hire young staff and train them in your image

Let's say you are to instigate a recruitment drive. Do you hire people with the right attitude and train them with the skill set that best suits your business? Or do you hire those who have the skills but might have the wrong attitude? Personally, I prefer to hire younger candidates, who are open-minded and eager to learn. These individuals develop, grow, learn and appreciate your philosophies and work ethic to a greater degree.

Less experienced staff can be trained up to speed in about three months. They don't demand the higher salaries and their enthusiasm and willingness are more important to my business. I started my business with a team of juniors, but they've been given the opportunity to grow and multi-skill. As the business has grown, I've complemented these younger employees with more experienced people.

Part of my philosophy is to ensure that my staff members are at their best, so training is a vital part of growth and development. I encourage my staff to attend courses, which the company pays for, as I view it as an investment in their future as well as my business.

Keep it simple and don't overstaff

Small business owners often run their companies like a ship's captain, retaining full decision-making power and control over the smallest details. But, as companies grow into larger enterprises with hundreds of employees and multiple product lines, the CEO's role must evolve as well.

The CEOs of consistently successful companies give their subordinates a great deal of freedom to run their parts of the business.

There are some simple questions that can help uncover understaffing or overstaffing problems:

- Has the business model changed?

- Have there been major spikes in demand?

- Has the company gone through a round of layoffs?

- Is the company's overall productivity on target?

- Have skill levels changed over time?

Any good business management consultant will tell you not to overstaff merely to impress clients, friends or family. Your bottom line is your profit and loss statement, not your staff complement. While there is a plethora of critics against multi-tasking, in the early stages of your business development and perhaps even into the next level of your evolution, staff capable of and willing to multi-task may not only be a benefit but could prove to be essential.

The most important point here is to grow your staff complement commensurate with your business needs, income and available capital; be flexible when it comes to considering part-time, casual and consultancy staff; but at the same time don't be penny-pinching and hold back on staff expansion when the genuine need does arise.

A big component of success is running a tight ship.

Do you have cash flow? Are your overheads too high? They are the factors you need to examine.

Don't overcapitalise on the assumption that your business is going to grow. Instead, once your business has grown, then spend the money. You've got to build the business one step at a time.

To enable me to run a tight ship, I have my staff multi-task wherever feasible. For example, all my salespeople are trained to complete costing sheets and purchase orders. I want them to know who the suppliers are and then I have them follow up the production. They can't be great salespeople if they don't know enough about production. A great salesperson can go into a meeting and answer questions on the spot. By multi-skilling, I can hire less staff. More importantly, it also means my employees are better informed as to how the business operates as a whole.

Make your operation look as big as possible, without lying about it

How you position your business is important. When I was starting DKM from the garden shed, I always tried to give the impression that I was a more established company to give people confidence when dealing with me.

Some of the ways you can 'fake it 'til you make it' include:

Always use the term 'we' rather than 'I':
One of the more subtle ways to look bigger than you are is to outsource your work and then refer to the outsourcer when talking to clients. If a client is asking you to complete some work and you say, "I'll have to check with my designer to see when I can get that to you," it sounds a lot better than, "I'm swamped this week, I'll try

to get to it when I can." You also can say that you have several people working in your business.

Create a professional logo:

A professional logo is more than a want — it is a necessity. Your logo represents you and your company to customers and partners. A customer may never step foot into your office, but they will definitely see your logo. The more professional it looks, the more professional you and your business look. If you don't have in-house expertise, someone at a logo design company can create a custom logo for your business. Start with your own idea or have design experts create one for you. Once you have the right logo, the design company can apply it to business cards, stationery, signage and more.

Create a professional website:

Having a website is a must for businesses today. A well-designed website can dramatically increase your business. Potential customers judge your business on both the design and functionality of your website. Also, ensure your content is grammatically correct and updated regularly. There are many web designers and online services to create and host savvy, professional sites at an affordable price. Remember, a well-designed website will attract new customers and keep old ones coming back. Design isn't the only consideration when creating a website. Make sure you have a respectable domain name, preferably your business name. Avoid using free sites to host your website as the website address will include the host site's name. Instead, register your own domain name and pay for your website hosting through any one of the reasonably priced hosting sites. A good domain name offers credibility to your company and makes it easier for customers to find you when searching the web. You can find out more about hosting your website and registering your domain name online.

Developing professional marketing materials:

Like your website, your print materials should also be top-notch. There's no reason this must cost a fortune. Simple tactics such as using heavy paper or card stock, or glossy paper instead of matte, can make a two-colour print job look like a high-quality one. Freelance designers often design stationery, business cards and marketing materials for less than half the cost of a traditional advertising agency. Also, you can save money by having the designer send you the final project files and then printing it yourself on a high-quality colour printer or copier.

Hire office space for important meetings:

Many small business owners work out of the home or in a one to two-room office, which isn't conducive for larger business meetings and presentations. But you can still have meetings with potential investors, vendors or customers over lunch or by renting meeting rooms in hotels or local office buildings. You can rent a meeting room for a specified number of hours a month for ongoing meetings and presentations. Renting a formal executive suite can give your company a professional appearance and make your business seem bigger than it is while allowing for a temporary solution to spending big bucks on your own luxury meeting facility.

Using some of the above tips will help boost your business appearance while saving money.

The best part is that you can work from home while projecting a professional image in keeping with your future membership in the Fortune 500!

Compete for awards

Business excellence awards, large or small, are often overlooked when it comes to marketing, yet they can really help stimulate customer interest. These awards are operated by a wide variety of organisations. Entering an awards program will usually require a brief essay and a description of your business. Some contests require financials. Entry is often free and when there is an entrance fee, it is normally not much.

"But I'll never win," you say. So, what? Even a nomination can bring many rewards.

Chapter 6 The Fledgling

Selling your products and services in today's competitive marketplace is tough. A business award win or nomination can act as a third-party endorsement. The added credibility can even be used as a sales closer. There is substantial anecdotal evidence to suggest that companies that win awards achieve sales growth of more than 35% more than non-winners. All companies profit from extra public relations. Awards are celebrations of achievement and hard work and a great story opportunity for the press to highlight small business. Not only that, but savvy employees want to work for the best companies. Corporate awards validate your hiring stature among new recruits.

Business awards offer many benefits to enhance your business's performance and profile, and are not something to shy away from. While not everyone can be a winner, half of the chance of winning is in the entering and, whether you win or not, the entire experience from penning the first word of the application to the awards ceremony and dinner can be an excellent reflective experience.

As the world's business environment becomes increasingly competitive and businesses question their return on investment for their marketing dollar, the strategic value of entering business awards can be an excellent way to gain a competitive edge over your competitors while increasing your profile and opening the door to further opportunities.

Hollywood stars vie for an Oscar. Musicians vie for a Grammy or an Aria. So why shouldn't you, as an ambitious, driven, savvy business owner, vie for your slice of the accolades too?

Though not as massive as it once was, a win or nomination at the Oscars still brings not only recognition of the highest accolade for professional talent, but a solid future of movie and TV contracts as well as a marked increase in earnings.

And the films themselves can generally expect a big uplift in takings too. A recent Ibis World report suggested that an Oscar nomination translated into a 25% increase in earnings for movies. So why is it that time and time again small business owners shy away from business competitions? It's time to reconsider.

Notes

Chapter Seven

Branded: *Thinking Outside The Box*

One of my main goals has been to be perceived as a market leader. To this end, I launched my own magazine, *Branded*.

Branded was an idea that came to me when I was speaking with the editor of *Marketing Magazine* during a tradeshow in Sydney. I was investing some money in advertising and wanted to push features and articles in their publication.

My aim is always to find how to invest next to nothing to generate something.

I was looking at ways to get exposure for my business and position myself as a market leader. I needed to put myself out there if I wanted to succeed. I came up with the idea of creating a magazine centred on the importance of branding. I wanted to redefine the way the industry was perceived in the marketplace and, in doing this, generate increased exposure for my business.

I intended to forge my position in the industry as a market leader in the branding, management and marketing arena. I wanted *Branded* to be a magazine that educated marketing managers about the importance of below-the-line marketing and branding.

After analysing the cost associated with the publication and how I was going to distribute it, we calculated that 16 pages would be the most cost effective size to produce and distribute. This would include a feature article written by me, some case studies and, to cover costs, some advertising space.

The overall cost of the publication was estimated to be $20,000 per issue. That included distribution, design, editing and printing 30,000 copies, making it the highest circulating magazine of its kind in the marketing industry. I piggybacked two leading publications and made *Branded* an insert in both. I arranged a group meeting with my key suppliers and pitched why they should advertise in my magazine. None of my suppliers sell directly; they rely on resellers to move their products to corporate companies. Their websites are generic ones that don't link back to their businesses. My angle was that this would provide a way for my suppliers to push their websites and products to end consumers, to force resellers to push their products. Eight advertisements at a rate of $2,500 for a full-page advertisement would cover my costs. My suppliers saw what I was trying to achieve and wanted to support my business just as I supported them. Funded through this advertising, my magazine became self-run with no expense to DKM, but it gave me scope to promote my philosophies and theories on business, and to share valuable case studies with consumers.

It was received with open arms, and DKM's credibility soared as more and more marketers read the magazine. It was a quarterly magazine. I felt this frequency was ample. I didn't want to flood the market and tried to anticipate any pressure that my suppliers might have on their advertising spend.

I also knew there would come a point where suppliers would need to pull back on their investments. Eventually, suppliers couldn't measure a direct result of spending the amount of money I was charging, as there was no actual direct sell other than the promotion of their websites and a few product images. I emphasised to them they should see this as more of a brand platform position. I would need to work out how to show my suppliers a return on their investment. I revisited my initial concepts and decided to turn the magazine into a 'product-and-article' driven business. Instead of just making *Branded* a stand-alone magazine, I drew a direct link to DKM and made it a direct sales magazine instead. The marketing articles and my feature column remained. I began convincing suppliers that the measure of their return on investment through sales was linked directly to DKM, and, if they invested in a full-page advertisement of products then DKM would elevate them to the top priority supplier within their category. Indirectly, the message was that, if they didn't support the next phase of *Branded*, they could lose DKM's support of their business.

I looked at *Branded* like any commercial magazine publisher would. If you want to promote your product, then you need to pay us for the advertising space to sell it. My focus now was to illustrate to my suppliers the math behind their investment. If they took out a full-page advertisement, it would promote up to eight products. With a circulation of 30,000, each advertiser would pay just eight cents per copy, which made it a very economical and attractive proposition for all. My first rollout with this new theory generated DKM $130,000 in new business. Our suppliers saw a direct link to sales as we could monitor the return on investment. Today, suppliers are soliciting me to request advertising space in *Branded*.

It was a real joy to see my ideas come to fruition. Believing in your theories and putting them into practice creates a strong sense of pride. Not every idea will work the way you expect it to, but you can't test your theories if you don't put yourself out there. *Branded* gave me the platform to put myself out there and voice my theories within an industry where I was determined to be a leader.

Branded was the first industry magazine to talk about the importance of marketing and branding, and was yet another technique I found to redefine my position in the industry.

Entrepreneurial Strategies — Chapter Seven

- Piggyback other distribution channels

- Think outside the box

- Don't aspire to the market standards — create your own and raise the bar

Piggyback other distribution channels

There is no 'one size fits all' here. I was able to very successfully piggyback the distribution of my magazine, *Branded*, by inserting it in other magazines that already had a distribution channel in place. Production and distribution of the magazine ultimately derived from selling advertising space.

While there may be similar opportunities available to you, if you consider your product or service and short, medium and long-term objectives, then this particular idea may not be suitable. Accordingly, let's look at a few other forms of distribution.

A firm's distribution objectives will ultimately be related to services versus goods and high-end versus low-end markets. For example, more exclusive and higher service distribution will generally entail less intensity and lesser reach. Cost trades off against speed of delivery and intensity (it is much more expensive to have a product available in convenience stores than in supermarkets, for example). The extent to which a firm should seek narrow (exclusive) versus wide (intense) distribution depends on a number of factors. One such factor is the consumers' likelihood of switching brands and their willingness to search out new brands. For example, most consumers will switch soft drinks rather than walk from a vending machine to a convenience store several blocks away, so the intensity of distribution is essential. Alternatively, if the product in question is sewing machines, consumers will expect to travel to a department or discount store and premium brands may have more credibility if they are carried only in full-service specialty stores.

Retailers involved in a more exclusive distribution arrangement are likely to be more loyal, that is, they will tend to recommend that product to the customer and thus sell large quantities. In its early years, Compaq instituted a policy where their computers had to be purchased through a dealer. On the surface, Compaq passed up the opportunity to sell large numbers of computers directly to large firms without sharing the profits with dealers. On the other hand, dealers were more likely to recommend Compaq since they knew that consumers would buy these from dealers. When customers came in asking for IBMs, the dealers were more likely to indicate that, if they insisted, they would sell them an IBM, adding, "But first, let me show you how you will get much better value with a Compaq."

Think outside the box

Don't struggle for a tiny niche. Instead, expand your horizons to create a whole new market opportunity.

The first principle is to reconstruct market boundaries to break from the competition. The challenge is to successfully identify how you can differentiate your business from your competitors. Don't compete on price but on your point of difference. DKM is different from other merchandising companies because we think like an ad agency rather than as a logo printing service. This is what makes us stand out.

The more companies compete on standard differentiators such as price, the greater the competitive convergence between them. To break out of stagnant waters, companies must break out of the accepted boundaries that define how they compete. Instead of looking within these boundaries, business owners must look systematically past such boundaries to create new opportunities. They need to look across alternative industries, strategic groups, buyer groups, and complementary product and service offerings. They also need to consider the functional and emotional orientation of an industry. This helps to give a company insight into how to open innovative offerings in the market.

In the broadest sense, a company competes not only with the other firms in its industry but also with companies in those other industries producing alternative products or services. For example, a book publishing company not only competes with other book publishers but also with the movie industry as an alternative entertainment source.

What are the alternative industries to your industry? Why do customers trade across them?

Focus on the key factors that lead buyers to trade across alternative industries and eliminate or reduce everything else; this can create a new market space for your business.

Always think outside the box. Start today.

Don't aspire to the market standards — create your own and raise the bar

If you want to lead the market, you must be the industry leader in developing new business models and new products or services. You must be on the cutting edge of new technologies and innovative business processes. Your customer value proposition must offer a superior solution to a customer's problem, and your product must be well differentiated. Also, you need to move faster than your competition! You must pursue the correct competitive strategy — avoid the strengths of your competitors and look for the weak points in their positions. Launch your marketing attacks against those weak points.

Then you need to sustain competitive advantage by implementing a unique, value-creating strategy based on a unique combination of organisational capabilities that cannot be replicated by competitors. It is this advantage that enables your business to survive against its competition over a long period. Do you want to encourage extraordinary performance from your people? Do you want them to do great things? If yes, then you must create an inspiring corporate culture to inspire and energise them. Your competitive advantage should excite your people and create that energy.

Serving your market means that you are actively involved on the micro-level and have an obvious, vested interest in that market. It is going the extra mile to identify solutions and engineering innovative methods to deliver those solutions.

Obvious benefits to serving your market and becoming a market leader include increased exposure, higher response and conversation rates and gaining unsolicited word-of-mouth referrals across the social media landscape. The latter is the best type of exposure possible.

Here are my keys to becoming a market leader:

- Becoming a market leader is the end result, not the goal: Becoming a market leader is not about having the largest mailing list, the highest-priced product or the biggest profit margin. Many businesses approach their market from that angle head on, not realising that these things are a result of market leadership. If you properly serve your market, then your list will naturally grow, and your products and services will ultimately be in higher demand. There is a difference between dominating your niche purely for gain and making every effort to truly serve your market. That difference is obvious to your clients and customers, and it dictates whether your success will be long-term in that market — or a flash in the pan.

- Become actively involved in your niche; be active on your sites and also across the internet. Reply to emails. Respond to blog comments. Create social media profiles and actively participate. Join niche discussion forums and contribute value.

- Create a customer follow-up strategy: Go beyond making the sale and create a follow-up strategy that encourages your buyers to consume the material and to experience results. Your vested interest and continued support will turn those buyers into a loyal customer base.

- Build a community, not a list: Don't simply build a list you can constantly market to; instead, build a community within your target market. Being a market leader means being a market listener and then taking action.

- Follow market trends: Don't be stale with your offer. Be proactive and move forward consistently — lead!

- Don't respond, initiate: While you should always respond to issues and conversations within your niche, you want to be the person to initiate those conversations whenever possible. Market leaders initiate relevant discussions.

- Be proactive, not passive: Reading a blog post is passive. Writing a blog post is proactive. Listening to podcasts is passive. Creating podcasts is proactive. Get actively involved in your niche by publishing content in a variety of formats across various media.

- Communicate frequently: Don't email your list only when you have something to sell them. Provide quality content on a regular basis to stay fresh in their minds. Consistently serving your market will build rapport and their trust.

- Act on feedback: show appreciation for the feedback you receive by acting on it. Acknowledge complaints and make necessary changes. While you don't want to become a slave to your market, you should open yourself up to serving that market when they make it a point to let you know how you can best do that.

How many of your competitors follow even half of the points on this list? How many of these points are you using in your business model? Take these ideas and dominate your niche simply by better serving your market.

Notes

Chapter 8

Stepping Into The Pop World

Success is not for the faint-hearted, and as in all things, there is a universal and cosmic balance. If you are not grateful for the success you achieve, not just in recognising your friends and those who helped you along the road, but in giving back to others in some meaningful way, you may discover that something will reverse your good fortune. I was determined this wasn't going to happen to me.

In 2004, I realised I needed to seek ways to differentiate myself from the competition. I felt one way I could do this was to extend the concept of branding merchandise to brand management by offering the kind of celebrity management services we are familiar with in the arena of sports and entertainment.

I wanted to stay involved in basketball and thought if I could become a player agent/manager, I could use my contacts in the sport to attract clients. Other than my common sense in business, I didn't know anything about being an agent. I don't know why I keep on throwing myself into the deep end and placing myself in situations I don't really know anything about.

The first player I managed was Kavossy Franklin, a highly talented American import who was part of the Sydney Kings first championship team but had recently returned to the USA as his contract had not been renewed.

Through the sport, we had a friend in common, and that friend confided in me that Kavossy was keen to come back to play in Australia the following year. Would I be interested in representing him? Kavossy and I met. Following our conversation, he was keen to see what I could do for him. As I wouldn't get paid if I was unable to secure him a contract, I didn't present a risk to him.

So I sounded out a few NBL clubs and generated some interest from The Hunter Pirates, who were based in Newcastle. This was my first experience with contract negotiation in the sporting arena. Even though I was a little bit nervous, I was excited to see what sort of deal I could negotiate. Kavossy had indicated he wanted more money than he had been getting from the Sydney Kings. I managed to negotiate a deal that would earn him $30,000 more. Needless to say, he was thrilled.

Not only did I manage to negotiate more money but I also managed to sign up his college teammate from

New Mexico, Clayton Shields. I had a college highlight reel that was four years old and used this to secure Clayton's deal. Clayton hadn't played in over two years, so he was excited about restarting his career. However, I was a bit scared as I was negotiating a deal for someone I hadn't seen first-hand and who had retired two years earlier. I had reservations about whether Clayton could, in fact, live up to expectations based on his college achievements. Unfortunately, a pre-season knee injury ended his hopes, and we never did find out how well he might have performed.

From then on, I didn't need to go searching for players to represent. Calls from Division One college players began coming in after Clayton spread the word. If I could sell Clayton based on old tapes, then these players wanted me to represent their interests. While I dabbled in this area of sports management for a little while, I didn't push it any further as I felt it required too much work for too little long-term loyalty to make this a worthwhile business. Instead, I redirected my focus back to merchandising and branding.

Then with the popularity of the television show, *Australian Idol*, a new and very different opportunity came my way. During its six-year run, the show launched many new careers globally. In Australia, as in other countries, hopefuls flocked to the auditions. Of those who did make it through, we saw astonishing, previously unrealised talent in our youth, but there is only one winner. What happens to the others? Some runners-up have gone on to enjoy success in the performing arts having realised their life's calling. How many of them, I wondered, fell prey to the hungry sharks that circled, waiting to pick off the cast-offs and the unwary?

One evening I was at my friend's restaurant when I was introduced to Cosima De Vito. Cosima had appeared in the first season of *Australian Idol* as a top three finalist and famously pulled out of the competition just before the final voting because of nodules in her throat.

On the back of the show, she went on to win an ARIA award and was the first independent artist to debut at No. 1 on the charts with her cover of Cold Chisel's, 'When the War is Over' which achieved platinum sales. Her first album went on to achieve Gold sales accreditation.

I suggested she should look at doing some merchandise, reasoning there could be some good opportunities for her. Cosima was there with her sister, Sarina, so I gave Sarina my card. I spoke with her a week later and organised a meeting. Cosima had started up her independent label called CDV Records, and my focus was on the merchandise possibilities of her career. An initial half-hour merchandising discussion stretched into a two-hour meeting, which spilled over into dinner and ultimately became a six-hour session. It was immediately apparent to me that there was a great deal more to Cosima than I had read about in the press. She was so much more interesting and talented than the negative publicity surrounding her quitting Idol suggested. She also revealed that her relationship with her manager was becoming strained.

What I knew about the music industry could have been written on a postage stamp, but I did know about running a business and managing a brand. Before long we agreed that I would start consulting with her on the business front. For the first time, I wasn't doing this work for any immediate gain; I simply felt sorry for her situation because she was raw in the business arena.

It was December 2004. We let the holiday season pass before settling down to any meaningful work. Then I began asking some serious questions.

When I asked Cosima later how I managed to earn her trust to step into such a pivotal position in her life, she told me that at the start she didn't like me; she thought I was arrogant.

However, after the first meeting, she said my apparent honesty changed her opinion. I wasn't trying to exploit her for money. Looking back, I calculate that I've probably spent more money on her career than I've made. Any other manager relying on her for an income would probably have left a long time before. But, unlike some of the sports stars I managed, I saw potential and talent in Cosima that she had yet to develop and it was this that made me want to help her.

There were times when I asked myself what I had got into, but I am not a quitter. Even if this wasn't about making money, it was about helping another human soul, which was rewarding and about challenging my boundaries, which was enriching.

Whether it is music or selling a product, the same business principles apply. These include managing your overheads, outgoings, and incomings. Selling artistic talent, though very subjective, is not different to selling a tangible product. Tangible or intangible, you still need to entice the consumer. Be it a song, an album, a photo, or a garment, the same principles apply. Once Cosima's massive outgoings were slashed, there came the point when her business interests were run out of my office and from there it was a short step for Cosima to ask me to manage her. There had been over a million dollars spent on producing and promoting Cosima's first album after *Australian Idol*. Cosima was not from a wealthy background; in fact, her parents had gone into debt to raise the money to support her dream. They didn't understand what the expenditures were for but assumed that, if people were spending that much money on Cosima, surely the returns would be enormous. The reality was, sadly, the complete reverse.

When I looked at all her invoices and saw what was being charged, I was staggered at how much money had been spent on public relations, promotions, rent, etc.

It was a learning curve for us both. For me, it was learning about the music industry. For Cosima, it was learning how to run her business and regain her belief that some people in business do have integrity. Even though I lacked knowledge and experience in the music industry, I had managed sports athletes before, and I had a few connections in the music business through various friends.

I began managing Cosima's expenses as well as her brand. I was testing my own abilities to see how far I could push my own boundaries in venturing into this new world. Perhaps the biggest challenge was managing a four-year legal battle against Cosima's ex-manager who was suing her for commissions and royalties of $500,000.

I involved my own lawyers, which was not cheap, to say the least. Together with Cosima, we worked out a plan. We knew Cosima's ex-manager didn't stand a chance. Finally, after four years of heartache, the judge ruled in Cosima's favour with a bill of only $40,000 to be paid for his unpaid work. Only then could she finally speak out, through exclusives in *New Idea* magazine and explain what had taken place.

The public battle took its toll on Cosima's career though. For a long time, even though Cosima and I knew that there was light at the end of the tunnel, that tunnel seemed awfully and interminably long.

I remained Cosima's manager for several years, and post the court case we put the blocks back in place to rebuild her career.

The difference with my management strategy was to make everything positive. I even secured her gigs with the legendary Demis Roussos, the hit musical *Hair* and booked her on a Roachford tour. Momentum returned.

This enabled me to manage the production of Cosima's second album, which we called, *This Is Now*. We worked on a budget of $100,000 compared to the million dollars squandered on her first album. My strategy behind the second album was ultimately to get Cosima back in the marketplace with a fresh new start and for us to create a bit of hype to generate corporate and live performances.

The intention was never to work toward record sales; after all, she no longer had the frenzy of *Idol* around her. I elected to produce a much smaller release of the overall album, 4,000 as opposed to 75,000 as she had done with her first. I wasn't looking at CD sales but at other areas. That strategy allowed us to recoup the album costs with live performances. Although it didn't sell a million records, we slowly and surely transformed her into a contemporary adult artist respected for her vocal talent.

Cosima penned six songs for her second album, making it infinitely more rewarding as she became part of the entire process. Under my guidance and management, she grew both as an artist and an individual, and developed a positive focus towards a bright future. As well as managing her, I took it upon myself to motivate her even though many people around me told me I was wasting my time and money. However, those critics don't know the real Cosima and couldn't possibly understand what we had gone through together as a team. Once again, they didn't share my vision and belief — well, that had happened before, so I just shrugged the criticism off. It was a real test, both emotionally and financially, but how can one put a price on keeping the dream alive?

My focus was on securing Cosima an income through live performances. All the emotional baggage was left behind, and we adopted the philosophy of the old saying, "What doesn't kill you makes you stronger." We both learned and grew through the tumultuous experience of a prolonged, high-profile lawsuit. Along with this, we bonded as friends who respected each other's knowledge of our respective fields.

Despite the roadblocks thrown up, we took the first step back to restoring the fallen idol to her throne.

Even when small things started to go well, I would keep Cosima grounded while maintaining my encouragement and positive attitude towards the future. I taught her how to look at everything from a business perspective, something she'd never done in the past.

The change in Cosima's brand was how we secured a national tour with the late Demis Roussos, a ten-time platinum artist. Performing at the Opera House and every other major venue in Australia has been a wonderful experience for Cosima. Even more amazing was that at the Opera House she was able to perform a song that she wrote when she was 11 years old, 'Forever Young.'

Cosima explains how much this tour meant to her: "I remember when we did the Demis Roussos tour; Dorry took me to the office and said, 'I've got a surprise for you.' He knew my Dad used to play his Demis Roussos album when I was a baby, and there was a song called 'Smile,' written by Charlie Chaplin that I would sing along to. Every time I would cry, Dad would rock me in his arms to Demis Roussos. Anyway, between Dorry and the promoters, they spoke to Demis and told him this story, asking him if he would be prepared to sing a duet with me, and he said, 'Absolutely.' So, there I was, on stage with a man who I have idolised my entire life, singing 'Smile.' I didn't think it could get any better than that, but after the tour had finished, Dorry gave me a blow-up of the Demis Roussos Opera House poster on an enormous plaque. He was so proud of it, and I thought it was an absolutely amazing gesture. After that, everything just flew. I headlined the musical *Hair* in Perth for three weeks, which was a sell-out show. Not only was it a sell-out but also the show was actually extended. And if that wasn't enough, Dorry negotiated a deal whereby I would earn a certain amount per show plus a bonus based on ticket sales which, combined, equated to an amount approximately seven to eight times what the other headline acts were making."

"We did the second album on a tenth of the budget of the first because, when it comes to negotiating, Dorry is absolutely fierce. The producer on it was Trevor Steel, who used to be with The Escape Club and most of the songs I recorded on it I'd written myself because Dorry told me I had to make money from this second album and to do that, they had to be my own original songs. So, that's what I did. I wrote most of the album, and when the first single, 'Keep it Natural,' was released as a dance version, we gave it to all the clubs, and I debuted in the ARIA dance charts as a result."

Cosima charted in both the ARIA Independent Music charts, as well as the ARIA Dance charts with her track 'Keep it Natural'. The gay community welcomed that track into their clubs with open arms and hearts, and the album started to sell in record numbers. I had recognised this as a niche market for Cosima and worked it. Releasing dance tracks off the album really worked wonders. Through 2007 and 2008, Cosima became a beloved gay diva, headlining the Sleaze Ball, which, after Mardi Gras, is the second biggest gay party in Sydney. She retains her popularity as a much-loved artist within the gay community, and that is all because I said I needed Cosima to develop a niche market.

Cosima was the first independent artist to debut at number one with 'When the War is Over,' which actually came from her first album but she didn't receive the award until 2005 when she was under my management. I escorted her to the ARIA No. 1 Chart Awards, and she handed me the award to keep in my office as a thank you for my support.

I adopted a specific and deliberate strategy concerning Cosima's second album. I knew Cosima's income stream would come predominantly from live performances. I would negotiate a fee for each performance equal to what she might earn for an estimated 1,000 album sales. Behind this rationale was the knowledge that all the hype from the TV show had been well spent. Yes, we needed product in the form of recordings for leverage at the performances to create credibility for Cosima as an artist and demand for future performances, but the strategy remained firm to sell Cosima as a live act, off the back of which the product sales would come.

Success isn't always a monetary thing. It's not about selling a million records. It can also be defined as facing challenges and working through obstacles. We faced a lot of challenges in that area, and we overcame them. Not everything you do is going to be outrageously successful. However, if your actions are undertaken with integrity and quiet confidence, you are moving ahead on the right track. Success is measured in many ways. Whether it's a small achievement or a big achievement, it's an achievement. The aim is to test yourself and to push beyond the barriers of perceived limitation. It's about having small goals and conquering them step-by-step.

Entrepreneurial Strategies — Chapter Eight

- Create your own benchmarks

- Be grateful and give back

- What doesn't kill you makes you stronger

- Branding is art, not a science

Create your own benchmarks

If you want to lead the market, there is no point in following what is currently the standard practice. Do what you think is right. When I started DKM, nobody was servicing the merchandising business the way we did or do now. We fitted in between an advertising agency and a promotional company, without the fees of an ad agency. That made us unique. People said it couldn't be done that way, but I knew I was right, so I followed that path.

As I said earlier, you should strive to be the industry leader in developing new business models and new products or services. Your customer value proposition must offer a superior solution to a customer's problem, and your product must be well differentiated. Also, you should move faster than your competition!

A market leader stands apart from other solution providers in their niche simply by listening more, providing higher quality, leveraging various elements in the market and simplifying processes. The bottom line is to become the 'go to guy' in your industry and to establish trust and rapport with your target market.

One of the keys to becoming a market leader is to examine your competition and determine what they are doing right. How can you do it better? Even more powerful is to determine what they are doing wrong (or not doing at all) and then to capitalise on that space between them and the market.

Be grateful and give back

You don't have to be Bill Gates and donate millions of dollars to charity to give back. To be grateful in life, all you have to do is to stay alert, watch your surroundings and not take life for granted.

Particularly once you become successful, you've got to stay humble and do things that are not always about money. With Cosima, my initial motivation was simply to help someone I could see was in trouble. By doing that, I've gained so much in terms of broadening my experience. You've got to learn to take on challenges and to keep pushing yourself beyond your boundaries. The moment you get complacent is the moment you stop growing. What doesn't kill you makes you stronger.

How often do we let the little things get in our way? In the course of our existence, we will each, no doubt encounter devastating losses, heartbreaking experiences and tumultuous issues. In those moments, when our concentration is focused on overcoming obstacles or coping with loss, we may be distracted from recognising what we can achieve. Feelings of loss only occur when there is an appreciation for the thing that is lost. You cannot lose what you never had.

Understanding what you can attain may cause frustration when encountering delays, but do not allow temporary interruptions to distract you from your personal goals. Learn from the obstacles and adjust accordingly. Just take a moment and remind yourself of what you can achieve. Small setbacks are insignificant in comparison to what you can accomplish and should never dissuade you from your course of action.

Most of our disappointments are the result of discovering that expectations or assumptions we had were incorrect. Occasionally, the realisation may have life-changing consequences. It is common to encounter such challenges in relationships, careers, and personal development.

Study the obstacles presented to you and adjust your course accordingly. In taking a new path, you will inevitably encounter new discoveries that you would otherwise have missed, both in the environment around you and within yourself. By overcoming a seemingly insurmountable situation, you could make a monumental discovery about yourself. Temporary setbacks and challenges cannot beat you, but you can use them to make you stronger. Everyone has heard the axiom, "Necessity is the mother of invention," meaning that, if everything was stable in everyone's lives all the time, there would be no progress or development in medicine, in technology, in philosophy or even in interpersonal relationships. Think of how many relationships have grown stronger through shared adversity.

There are countless examples of historical and global significance where almighty adversity has led to monumental and positive developments. But, on an individual level, suffice to say that the mind is stronger than anything, so much so in fact that it does have the ability to either kill you or make you stronger. Developing inner strength is what is directly responsible for developing outer strength. If a challenge is sent to you to overcome, don't walk away from it or you'll never know what treasures lay behind the door you forever left unopened.

Branding is art, not science

I believe brands are one of the most, if not the most, important assets for any business. I can understand why finance departments want to measure their value. But there is an important point that the whole 'value' argument misses: brands are all about emotional responses, things such as trust, confidence, image, and values. You can't measure these things.

To use an Australian example, Gough Whitlam's government paid AUD$1.3million in 1973 to purchase, 'Blue Poles' by Jackson Pollock, which at the time caused public outrage at the extravagant government spending. Fast forward to 2016, when the painting was valued at $350 million; a great investment by any standards. However, if thought about in material terms, the actual materials to produce the painting would probably cost under $1000. Even if Pollock had charged the original buyer for the hours spent on the artwork it would not rationally make the painting worth so much. But, people and governments do not buy art for rational reasons. It's art after all.

People pay for art based upon how it makes them feel. They pay because art evokes an emotional response and people place value on the experience of feeling emotion.

An artist, especially one like Cosima, is all about the emotional connection they make with their audience. An executive at a record company might measure the value of an artist in terms of record sales but this misses the point.

For example, when Cosima was a special guest for Demis Roussos's national tour and performed at venues such as the Opera House, there was obviously a hard commercial value that could be drawn from the event. There was an appearance fee plus the chance to build profile and CD sales.

But these transactions were not directly linked to Cosima's value as a performer. Her value is immeasurable because it begins and ends with the emotional response Cosima's performance evoked within each member of the audience.

How do you measure that?

The work I do with brand management is the same. The value of a brand is wholly contained within the emotional response it solicits from its audience. That is their essence. That is why brands are so incredibly valuable.

Some business leaders judge anything that cannot be reduced to a financial transaction as having no value. But this hard-line perspective is their limitation, not a limitation on the part of professional brand managers. If a CEO or CFO sees no value in their brands, then it is their loss; ultimately their brand values will be eroded, and their whole business will wither accordingly.

I can't put a hard dollar value on what I experience when I hear a live performance by a great artist. Whatever it costs to attend, to me it's worth it. Would I resell my ticket for $500, or even $1000? Even thinking about the emotional value in this way alters my perspective and diminishes the experience somewhat.

Marketing and brand managers typically have an intrinsic understanding of the value and importance of brands. All the hyper-rational talk about fixing exact dollar values to brands does not help define brand value except for those executives who only think in terms of hard currency.

We could argue that if they don't get it, then it's their problem. But that is ultimately defeatist. We all have to work together. We are all on the same team. At the end of the day everyone, from the most junior right up to the most senior, is measured by the overall performance of their organisation.

I strongly believe that marketing managers should be referred to as relationship managers. As custodians of our brands, we are the ones ultimately responsible for ensuring everyone is rallying to protect our standard and winning new ground.

Notes

Chapter 9

The Sydney Kings: Chasing A Dream

For me building success is always challenging but even more challenging is maintaining it. As I've said before, I have always had a passion for basketball and the Sydney Kings was the team that I loved as a child.

I think most men dream of being associated with a sport in some shape or form. I was fortunate to follow my dream and have a crack at investing in one. Did I think it was a money-maker? Of course not! Did I think I would lose money doing this? Of course I did.

It was at a time in my life when I had accumulated some personal wealth, and the sport was going backwards. I knew that certain clubs were going through tough times. I made a call to a friend and ex-player, Derek Rucker. That call led to a meeting with Robbie Cadee, CEO of the West Sydney Razorbacks. Robbie had been there for ten years and was a veteran of the sport. We struck up an instant rapport and were soon looking at how I could invest in the second Sydney team. A deal was nearly struck with the Razorbacks but I was pipped at the post by another investor.

The team where my heart really belonged was, of course, the Sydney Kings but I hadn't believed the Kings would be interested in investors, hence my focus on the Razorbacks. I was just about ready to forget the whole thing when I received a call from Derek saying the Kings wanted to talk. As I'd always had a soft spot for the purple and gold, I didn't need to be asked twice.

Negotiations began looking positive. It was clear to everyone this was potentially a good marriage of skills and experience. Tim Johnston owned the team, and I took a 10% share.

I knew I would lose money and I knew how much money I was willing to lose to live out a dream. Even though I knew I would not make money directly from the sport, I had an idea that I could use the professional sporting arena as a vehicle to diversify into other corporate environments, cross-pollinate my business and make them leverage off each other.

People thought I was mad investing in the team and said it was a waste of time; I agree they were right on one level, but they didn't understand what I was trying to create.

I looked at my investment as a marketing exercise. The perks I had with my part-ownership included promoting my company through courtside advertising, courtside corporate boxes and displaying my logo on all team uniforms and merchandise. I was able to manage and purchase the stock through my business. I was also able to promote my artist, Cosima, during warm-up and game time as part of the entertainment schedule. At the very least, if I entertained corporate clients and networked through the channels of the Kings, I would likely gain business from the endeavour and give my company, DKM, exposure. I started putting DKM everywhere and leveraging off each of my networks and brands to benefit the others.

It's natural for me to look at ways and possible opportunities to help any part of my business to grow through my ventures. This appeared to be a win-win scenario for both my business and me.

I received a phone call from the team's coach, Brian Goorjian, welcoming me and saying how excited he was to have me on board. I have a lot of respect for Brian. He is one of the most motivational people I have ever encountered and has the funniest personality. He is, in my opinion, the greatest coach in the history of the NBL and the friendship we built up over the year I was involved with the Kings still endures.

Brian had this to say about his time with the Sydney Kings:

"When the Kings changed ownership, from this time on, the uniforms for the players, the practice games, the training facilities, the contracts and the promotion of the game were bad. I had been around for a long time, so I was naturally concerned at what I was seeing. It is my recollection that it was at about this time that Dorry walked into my life. There was no one from the ownership around us, there was no support, there was no anything, and then all of a sudden Dorry walked through the door, and I was told that he was going to be part of the ownership of the team. From the moment I met him, in all honesty, he provided me comfort. Here was a guy that was young, full of energy, positive, very intelligent, motivational, innovative and charismatic. If you had a business contact, you could be confident that Dorry could talk about any subject. He was confident; he was comfortable with himself, and he was impressive. He could relate to the players because he'd been a player himself. He would make you feel positive, even when the environment was negative. He was a can-do guy. If Dorry was buying uniforms, you knew they were going to be good quality. If attendance numbers were down, he had a four-pronged approach to building the numbers back up. I remember an unbelievable Christmas party with a lot of high flyers around. He brought many impressive people to the game. You could tell he was connected; he was a mover, he was aggressive. He was unbelievably positive in a completely negative environment, assuring us we were going to be okay, explaining what we were going to do in marketing and he was always at the games with high energy talking about the plans to move forward."

All this was new territory for me, and I was determined to cherish every moment of this and learn from it. At the first training session I attended, Brian introduced me to the team. We had a championship team with five Olympians in our squad. I introduced myself and gave the players some background on me, as this was the first meeting for most of us. I was the same age as most of these young players, so I had to try and earn their respect. Over the weeks I focused on building trust with Brian and the players. Actions speak louder than words in my book and I made every effort to ensure my actions spoke of my full support.

I invited family and a few close friends to sit in my courtside box at the first home game. I had a smile from ear to ear throughout the entire game thinking to myself this is one of the most unbelievable moments of my life. Apart from the nerves, the experience was both exhilarating and surreal. I kept thinking about how far I had come in such a short time and all the obstacles I had overcome to get me to this point. To share this experience with family and friends gave me a true sense of pride. My passion for the sport had brought me to this place that I created for myself, a place where I knew I was going to make a difference.

I had never forgotten the excitement that raced through my young veins when I was a towel boy for the Sydney Kings and part of me always dreamed of owning a piece of that club if I couldn't play for them professionally.

The 2007/08 season was one of the most challenging years in the history of the Sydney Kings, and it was this year that, by the season's end, we folded. I had been there at both the birth and the death of the Kings. Despite all the off-court drama, we managed to finish minor premiers and have the second best record in the history of the NBL with 27 wins and three losses.

How did it all go pear-shaped? It started with our major shareholder walking away from the team and his heavy investment. After that, each month it was a battle to stay afloat, with funds deposited into the accounts at the eleventh hour. The experience was probably the most challenging one I have ever encountered. To finish minor premiers was amazing, particularly considering all the off-court difficulties as things crumbled. Credit must be given to Brian, the coaching staff and the players. I did my best to support both the players and coaching staff, but I could see where it was going. As a minority holder, however, there was little I could do. For someone who prefers to be in control, it was difficult to accept that I could not fix what was wrong.

One of my rules I live by now is that I will not invest in something I cannot control. If I cannot control the situation, I don't want to be a part of it. If I am going to fail, I want to fail because of my own inability, not someone else's.

At my very first board meeting, just one week after I invested into the team, I could see there were serious issues that needed tackling. I was determined to view this as a challenge, not as an insurmountable problem.

It was at this meeting that I met Harry Cousens, a former Kings owner. We soon became good friends.

Harry is Sydney-born and bred, educated in a public school and entered the computer industry at a very young age. It was Harry who oversaw Dell Computers' entry into the Australian market in 1993, eventually becoming its managing director.

In 2000, year of the Sydney Olympics, he decided to take a six-month sabbatical during which time he decided to retire and enjoy getting to know his kids and relax.

However, aged just 42, he still wanted to be involved in the business world and looked around at possible investments. One area that particularly attracted him was sport. Harry is an absolute sports fanatic with favourite teams in every code.

Coincidentally, his cousin, Mike Wrublewski, had started the Sydney Kings in 1988 and so the family had a fondness for the team. Harry explains his involvement in the club:

"It was always a great night out with the kids. Saturday and Sunday nights we'd take the children to the Entertainment Centre. It became a family tradition so when an opportunity came past my nose regarding the then ownership group in 2004, to see if I would like to buy 10% of the club, I couldn't ignore it. I knew it wasn't a great financial investment; it was more of a lifestyle investment. When my friends asked, 'Ever think about buying a boat?' I'd say, 'No, I have a basketball team instead.' A boat wastes about the same amount of money as owning a sports team but, to me, it was much more enjoyable. It was rewarding in many other ways too, such as growing my network and getting to make very close friends with the likes of Brian Goorjian and Bill Tomlinson, the coaches of the club. We won three titles, so that was very satisfying, too."

"It was then that our CEO, Gordon Allen, who had realised the club was in financial difficulties, was looking for some other investors. Dorry was introduced to us. That was about September or October 2006. I met Dorry at his office the very first time when Gordon Allen organised a meeting between me, Tim Johnston, some of his people and Dorry. I thought as Dorry was running a successful business he could be an asset to the club. Of course, he didn't know me from a bar of soap, and I didn't know who this young boy was, but very soon we became very, very close friends. We bonded.

Chapter 9   The Sydney Kings: Chasing A Dream

We found each other to be honest and had common interests, chiefly in wanting to see the Kings do well. Even though those were tough times, Dorry knew what he was getting himself into and as he'd turned his own life around so remarkably to succeed in business I thought, well why can't he do it with basketball? Most people who love sport think they know how to run a sports team. Let me tell you that very few people know how to run a sports team. Sport is one of the toughest businesses to make money in, and the quality of sports management in this country is, in my opinion, abysmal. This is why we see a lot of sports entities in big trouble."

As enjoyable as the season was, it was also equally frustrating. I had no control over changing the issues I felt needed changing. I could see that things were going south but was powerless to stop this happening. Our back office was in disarray; our corporate sponsorship was minimal, and ticket sales were average. A lot of people involved seemed content just to be there, without rolling up their sleeves and getting their hands dirty. No one seemed to want to turn things around. Maybe they were simply out of their depth.

Our on-court performance was the best it had ever been. Brian had the team in sync and our early season trip to China to compete against Yao Ming and the Chinese national team, CSKA Moscow and Benetton Treviso, was a turning point. It instilled in us the belief that we could compete on the world stage against the best teams in the world. This trip away brought back many of my childhood fantasies. Childhood fantasies have a way of weaving their way into our adult lives. Here I was, sitting on the team bench, part of the Sydney Kings. Admittedly, it was not as a player, but to be present in that moment as a shareholder is a feeling I hope I never forget.

We were on the verge of winning the title. I was thrilled that we might win a title during my first season as a shareholder. It was regarded as one of the best series ever played. In Game Four, we came back from 22 points down to take it to Game Five at the Sydney Entertainment Centre. Sadly though, we went down in Game Five of the grand final against the Melbourne Tigers. Sadly, because of injuries we lost in the final minutes. Regardless, it was one of my most memorable nights to date. Two hours before tip-off we were sold out with 10,500 seats sold at the Sydney Entertainment Centre. The atmosphere was electric with the Sydney community coming together in support of the Kings. It was still a perfect ending to a season that many suspected would be the last.

At the season's end, serious issues began to arise. Players were no longer being paid because our major investor walked away. The media got a sniff of this, and before we knew it, the liquidators descended and seized the business to recoup what they could. I lost some money, but I had been prepared for that.

Harry and I went into survival mode, attempting a rescue plan to raise $1.5 million to keep the team alive but, after three weeks, we were still $600,000 short. I'm proud of what we managed to do in such a short time, but unfortunately, it wasn't enough.

Here is an article from the *Daily Telegraph* at the time:

Towel boy's bid to save Sydney Kings

By Tim Morrissey
From: Daily Telegraph
June 24, 2008

A FORMER Sydney Kings towel boy is putting together a business plan to revive the team he once wiped the sweat off the floor for — but has just 48 hours to do it.

Dorry Kordahi is behind a bid to buy the Kings and save the club from NBL extinction.

Kordahi has remained a passionate Kings fan since his court-wiping days in the 1990s and, with his business partner Harry Cousens, is behind a last-ditch bid to save them.

He held a 10% stake in the franchise owned by Tim Johnston, who has vanished, leaving a trail of debt and despair since the club's catastrophic collapse.

Like the unpaid players, coaches and staff, Kordahi, who owns a marketing company, was also badly burnt financially by Johnston but has been working frantically with Cousens to put a rescue package together.

Cousens, a successful businessman in his own right, was also a previous Kings owner with the consortium that sold the club licence to Johnston.

The pair has raised close to $1 million but need to find some more investors to bring in a further $600,000 if they are going to have a legitimate shot at taking over the Kings' licence. "The business plan is there, the NBL has been encouraged by what we've been able to put together in just four days," Kordahi said.

"We just need a couple more key investors to get this thing over the line to save the Sydney Kings."

If the pair cannot find the extra cashed-up investors within the next 48 hours, Kordahi and Cousens will recommend the contracted Kings players and coaching staff try to find a spot on other NBL teams. Even if the consortium does raise the money, there is debate about whether the new venture could keep the Sydney Kings name.

We could have invested more ourselves, but I wasn't willing to gamble the business I had created on a dream and risk losing it all. Controlled spending and not letting emotions get in the way of business decisions is the most important lesson I learnt from this experience.

Sadly, my dream only lasted one season and for a year or so the Kings ceased to exist as a professional team. But even in that short time, I believe I positively influenced a few people's lives along the way. Moreover, the Kings are back again, and I am still a great fan!

Of course, some were quick to criticise me for having lost money on my dream investment; however, I did secure new business out of my association with the Kings. So, from a purely clinical and financial viewpoint, the entire exercise actually turned out to be a good investment in marketing!

Entrepreneurial Strategies — Chapter Nine

- Spend wisely and prepare for the down times

- Connect (leverage) your networks

- Have small goals, as well as large ones

- Tough times call for smart measures

Spend wisely and prepare for the down times

One of my main business rules is to spend only to a point where I am not exposing myself to unnecessary risk. Also, I make sure that, when I do spend, I can leverage off it. I prepare for the down times by not spending all my money, which is why I've always believed in running a tight ship. When you run a tight ship, you have good cash flow. Then, if an economic tidal wave hits, you have the resources to weather the storm.

When people ask if I have experienced tough times in business, I can honestly state, "No, I haven't," the reason being that I've managed my cash flow well. I've analysed possible risks, and I've never exposed the business to the degree that it would be detrimental. By running a tight ship and having good cash flow, I can overcome any hurdle and take on any risk that comes my way. And so can you.

Connect (leverage) your networks

Most businesses don't have the brand name to generate significant revenue by cold selling. Therefore, leveraging off your network (or others' networks) to obtain clients is a viable method which is both beneficial and lucrative. It is critical to build relationships because you never know who knows who or how the dots will connect in a meaningful way for you. Over time, your relationships will generate greater success for you. Most entrepreneurs find their first few clients in this way.

To leverage your network, you need to take stock and find out who is in your network. Take the time to see who you know. Chances are you know more people than you realise. As you build relationships with people in your network, make sure that you also open up your network in return. It cannot be one-sided.

Building these relationships is important for several reasons. First, it is a great way to get a referral. In addition, your contacts might also have the inside track on any plans and opportunities within your industry. Remember that your main goal in networking is to learn as much as you can and determine your strengths in your industry.

What do you do if your network does not contain any relevant contacts for your business?

Work out how your networks can cross-pollinate. Remember how I used Cosima to sing at the Sydney Kings' games? It attracted celebrity to the basketball scene and increased Cosima's exposure at the same time. Who in your network can be cross-pollinated in this way?

Have small goals, as well as large ones

Not every venture you undertake must be a massive step forward. It's okay to take smaller steps, to have smaller goals, as long as you continue to move forward. With the Sydney Kings, my investment in the club didn't return any monetary value, but regarding exposure of the DKM brand, it sure did. I would have loved it if it had developed into success for the team; however, kicking some small goals is still satisfying.

If your venture misses even the smaller goals you set, there are ways to be prepared:

- Don't panic. Panic gets you nowhere.

- Keep learning. Learning from the bad times enables you to react quickly when negative circumstances occur.

- Realise that it is just money. When a crisis hits, shift your perspective towards the positive things in your life.

- The sun will still rise tomorrow. No crisis lasts forever.

Tough times call for smart measures

Client spending is, of course, affected by the economy. If clients buy, as most do, imported goods and the Australian dollar slides down 35% against the US dollar (the major international trading currency) then the unit costs of goods rise accordingly. Yet the clients' budgets remain the same. The result is smaller orders in terms of units. Essentially this means the supplier's turnover has been reduced by 35%.

In tough times many marketing managers will be faced with cuts. But smart companies increase their budgets at that point. It's tough to plan. Why? Because decisions must be made looking forward. It is much easier to make a reactive decision than a proactive one. During an economic downturn you will hear the words, "Sorry, there's nothing I can do about it. It's just the downturn."

Positioning your company and brand correctly in hard times can be the most profitable thing you can do, both in awareness and market share. Start forging strategic alliances with suppliers and customers alike. This will give you time to plan and budget effectively.

Customers and suppliers alike should be viewed as a long-term commitment. Giving your customers good value for money allows them to better use their budgets to get 'more bang for their buck.'

Notes

Chapter 10

What I've Learnt About Merchandising

Now I don't want this chapter to sound like a sales pitch, but I think it is important to realise that my success has stemmed from doing something against the grain and something that I believed in wholeheartedly. So, I want to reiterate where the promotional products business stood and how my vision differed from the existing view. Hopefully, you can use this knowledge when thinking about your own business plans.

Fifteen years ago, the promotional products and merchandising industry sat firmly at the bottom end of the marketing industry. It was all about cheap coffee cups, cheap water bottles, and cheap t-shirts.

When running an event or a campaign, promotional product purchases were left to the last minute, designed solely to soak up excess marketing budget — assuming there was any. Purchasing decisions were left to the junior office assistants who rang around for three quotes and went with the cheapest.

The approach resulted in the unfortunate association, in the minds of prospects and clients, of valuable corporate brands with products that not only looked cheap but were cheap.

The focus on cheap products reaffirmed the perception that the promotional products industry sat solidly at the low end of the marketing profession. It was a self-perpetuating belief that persisted for decades, right through the 1960s, '70s, '80s and '90s.

This perception has now begun to shift, on the back of some great ideas, and plain hard work, both of which have gone into recent campaigns and produced extraordinary results. There is a new professionalism emerging along with a new creativity.

Marketers are beginning to comprehend the strategic value of promotions and merchandising. In turn, promotional product agencies are responding by offering a more sophisticated level of service and output.

Suppliers are increasingly aware of their role in designing and supplying high-value brand platforms, as opposed to simply shipping container loads of cheap product in from China.

For example, take the sensational Boonie Doll campaign. In 2005, the Boonie Doll was part of a Victoria Bitter (VB) beer campaign. Offered for sale with a carton of the beer was a talking figurine of Australian cricketer David Boon that uttered comments when prompted

Chapter 10 What I've Learnt About Merchandising

by the cricket's television commentary. The technology involved was very sophisticated for the time as it relied on both computer chips and timing devices.

The Boonie Doll was a classic example of how to use a brand platform successfully. It captured the essence of the VB brand perfectly and delivered it into the hands and homes of beer drinkers everywhere.

The publicity was astounding. And although social norms have changed in the years since the campaign, the Boonie Doll is still remembered long after the TV ads and key sponsors are forgotten.

But remnants of the old world persist.

For example, we once received a phone call from the organisers of a major sporting event. The event was on a Sunday night. The phone call came in on the preceding Wednesday. To ensure the atmosphere was well and truly pumped, the event organisers wanted to hand out a free, promotional product as the crowd entered the stadium. We delivered. (We always do!)

What they got from us was a pretty standard giveaway for sporting events of all codes and significance. But you have to shake your head and wonder, what if they had taken a strategic approach and contacted us weeks earlier? What if, given a little more time and thought, they had been able to give away an item that was unique and captured the essence of their particular sport? One that people would keep and value?

It wouldn't have cost them extra. But it would have delivered a real punch that had a life above and beyond the event itself — just as the Boonie Doll did for VB as well as cricket in general.

I believe the brand platform business delivers great value to consumers, to marketers, to agencies and suppliers.

Good quality branding is all the more important today when many brands exist only in cyberspace or on television. Merchandising and promotional products may be the only time your customers come into physical contact with your brand.

The true value of any promotional idea is equal to the perceived value as seen by your customers. High quality and strong utility are just two portions of the equation. The real value your customers look for is confirmation that their trust in your brand is well placed.

So, let's examine more closely what 'value' is to your customer. What value do your prospective (and existing) clients perceive within your brands, products, and services?

Value is the single most important issue in the promotions business. Typically, people want to buy a product that costs as little as possible but is perceived as high value by their clients. 'Value' is discussed via criteria such as weight (heavy items not made of low-quality plastic) or usefulness (will people actually use the object?). Weight and usefulness are two great reasons why the ubiquitous coffee cup often wins the day. It is made of nice heavy ceramic and is useful around the office. The value discussion is often, however, only one-dimensional: "How much value will my prospect perceive this gift has?" A more important question is overlooked: "How will this product impact on the value of my brand?"

In the value stakes, nothing is more important than the value proposition wrapped up in your brand. Does the product add value to your brand? Does it diminish the value of your brand? Does it change the perceived value of your brand? What we can't do is lose sight of the real issue. Promotional products are brand platforms first and promotional gifts second.

Imagine for a moment that you work in marketing for a company hosting a conference in two weeks. You have some budget left over for a conference and want to find out the price of some 'giveaways.' Your intention is to get three quotes and then go with the cheapest. The question you need to ask yourself is this: In six months' time, what is the only physical object your delegates will have to remind them of your conference? The answer is, of course, the giveaway. Do you want the only lasting memory of your event to be the cheapest t-shirt or coffee cup that money can buy? By approaching promotional products differently, as a strategic buy, you can devise or design an item that is unique, that perfectly encapsulates your brand or your event, and is of real appeal and value to your target audience.

What you are buying, remember is a platform for your brand. Yes, to some extent the majority of promotional products suppliers have perpetuated the common misconception that cheap coffee cups, cheap water bottles, and cheap t-shirts are what it is all about. But in a fast-paced digital world, the value of an item that can be held in your hand, an item that lasts and can be used and treasured, becomes paramount. I have been at the vanguard of creating meaningful products for this market area and been rewarded by seeing things I created for a one-day event still in use many years after.

Think of the promotional products business as the 'brand platform' business. You have the opportunity to deliver to your customers some fantastic items that reflect your brand values perfectly, ones they will keep and prize. Would you rather see your brand represented on an attractive, quality item or a cheap coffee cup or plastic water bottle for the gym?

Entrepreneurial Strategies — Chapter Ten

- Brand quality is king

- Don't settle for poor customer service

- Get in early to get results

Brand quality is king

My belief in the value of good quality merchandise is why I continue working to elevate the profile of the industry. My goal is to place the industry front and centre in the marketing strategies of our leading corporations.

Why do I think branding is so important? The brand is arguably the most important asset of most businesses. Organisations spend millions building their brands and rely upon them to help sell their wares. Brands are useful tools because customers come to trust them as a guarantee of quality, as a guarantee that their expectations will be met and, ideally, exceeded.

That's why promotions and merchandising decision-making is crucial. Make the right choice, and your brand reaps the benefits. Make the wrong choice, and your reputation may be damaged, possibly irrevocably. Promotions and merchandising are about providing brand platforms — not just products, but ideas and concepts as well.

Within my company, we have a code: we add value to your brand, we protect your brand, we extend your brand, and we build your brand.

My business is based upon working with the client to understand their brand and making recommendations that sets their business apart, as well as cut through, reinforce and promote the client's chosen image.

At the end of the day, what customers want is reassurance that their growing confidence in your brand is well placed. Your customers want to trust your brand and to do so they must sense the existence of a relationship between them and you.

Don't settle for poor customer service

Great advice is an integral part of the customer service package. More than just a purveyor of promotional merchandise, my company is a valuable contributor to its clients' businesses, providing consultation services to achieve the best possible result for their brands. My philosophy is all about protecting and enhancing brands through strong management and smart merchandising, as well as providing great service and competitive prices.

The other key value is how the company makes a client feel. It's called good, old-fashioned customer service. And, believe me, it is invaluable.

Every business gives lip service to customer service: "Yes, yes," they say, "customer service is very important."

But do they really believe it enough to commit to it fully? If they don't believe it, perhaps it is because they don't fully understand the reasons behind why customer service is critical.

Let's look at some everyday examples. Telephone a large corporation, utility or finance company. More often than not, you will be connected to their call processing system and asked to make selections in up to four or more menu systems. You will hear messages telling you to continue holding, the recorded voice repeating that your call is important to them and how much they value your time. Really? Whose time do they actually value?

Call processing menus are designed to cut a company's costs by increasing call centre efficiency. Today, Australian call centre staff earn about 10% less an hour than the national average wage. Therefore, the call centre values your time as a below average commodity too.

You may wonder then; does customer service really matter all that much? Many companies appear to thrive despite offering terrible service. I should say though some companies have improved over the last few years with initiatives such as live chats, etc. But from the very outset, my business model dictated that customer service is to provide not only a fast turnaround but to take the time to understand the customer and what works for their business. I differentiated my business by putting an end to handing the customer a catalogue of standard, cheap (i.e., low value) promotional items. Make it your business truly to understand your customer and provide exceptional service.

Get in early to get results

In contrast to the temporary and costly nature of media campaigns, a good below-the-line campaign can deliver cost-effective items directly into your target market and leave your customer with a lasting reminder of your brand. But don't leave the details to the last minute. A good promotional merchandise company is every bit as creative as above-the-line agencies. You can't, however, expect to call a promotional products company regarding an event that's taking place in just three days' time and still get an exceptional, creative product. You must learn how to use the services of promotional product companies effectively. Promotional products can be innovative, fun and memorable; they can really drive a campaign when done properly.

Placing your brand on items with a high-perceived value shows that you care about both your customer and your brand by offering them something worth keeping and using for a long time to come. Every time they use that product they will be favourably reminded of your brand.

Quality does not necessarily translate to costly, but items, whether large or small, should be well designed and well manufactured. Perception is a very important part of delivering a great product campaign — it adds value.

Notes

The Last Dance: our Game Five of the NBL grand final, Sydney Kings vs Melbourne Tigers. The game sold out the Sydney Entertainment Centre even before tipoff, which hadn't happened in years.
Seeing those sold out signs in the foyer showed it was possible for Australian basketball to be as popular as the national obsessions of rugby and cricket

DKM courtside branding at the Sydney Entertainment Centre. This gave me the opportunity to leverage my brand against my other interests so all benefitted at the same time.

Adversity is character building
Brian Goorjian, probably the greatest coach ever in Australian basketball.
We faced some very tough challenges during our time with the Sydney Kings. But despite this our friendship not only endured but has remained rock solid to this day.

Building on Australia's rich manufacturing history. Ambassador's founders Frank and Esser Chahoud in their Belmore NSW factory circa 1944.

The DKM Blue Showroom today. One of the largest of its type in Australia. A place not only for display, but a meeting hub for customers to thrash out solutions with our design and sales teams

A great experience! Being recognized and appearing on Network Ten with Australia's Entrepreneurial Luminaries.

The unlikely source of me becoming involved in women's fashion. Publisher, aviator and philanthropist Kevin Weldon AM.

Diversification
The company's move into the fashion world has allowed it to establish an exceptional stable of fashion brands and made it unique among its competitors. I believe diversification is the key to growth.

Working on all aspects of my business. Behind the scenes with Danny at one of our fashion shoots — it's all in the detail!

When I first visited Shanghai in 2002 to meet my Chinese business partner Jimmy the city was nothing like the 24/365 bustling place it is today. It was a real struggle to make my mark in such a closed market. Nevertheless I succeeded and that footprint has given my company a real head start over its competitors.

Increasing and consolidating my footprint in China — pictured recently with Chinese business associate, former Alibaba senior executive Jackie Wang.

Over the years DKM Blue parties have given us an opportunity to thank our partners and clients for their continued loyalty and support.
As they have grown bigger and bigger our guests have become like a giant family!

Chapter 11

Don't Slash and Burn: Cost Control And Planned Growth

In 2008, as most will remember, a financial tsunami which became known as the 'GFC' hit all the economies of the Western world and impacted on many others.

Surprisingly, the GFC had a direct and very positive effect on me. I have said before that we should all look for silver linings in the darkest of clouds. That is what my brother, Danny, and I did in 2008.

Back then, Danny's business, DK Blue, was focused on corporate uniforms and online platforms to sell and distribute, while my company, DKM, focused on direct importing, marketing, and merchandising.

Everyone, but everyone was looking to save costs at that time. However, simple cost cutting can have a detrimental effect on a company's structure, culture, and viability. Making cost cuts is just the same as any other strategic decision; it can be good or bad. So yes, cut costs when it's a matter of efficiency, but be careful not to 'slash and burn' because that can send out some very bad messages — to staff and clients alike. And if staff morale is low because of it, that will be noticed by clients too.

So, Danny and I started discussing how we could make our businesses leaner without affecting staff and clients. In fact, we not only wanted to make our companies leaner, but we also wanted to make them better and stronger than they were before.

What did the two companies have in common? Well, they both sold things to similar sorts of companies. They also transported those same things, invoiced them, and warehoused them. It wasn't like trying to merge a shipyard building supertankers with a nursery growing orchids on a commercial scale.

We realised we could seriously reduce our joint expenditures by putting nearly every aspect of our respective businesses under a single management and administrative system. Not only that, we could even put them both in the same building!

Moreover, most of our existing clients would likely want the various products and services we sold previously but separately provided.

We could not only save money; we could streamline efficiencies and increase sales in one fell swoop.

Despite being a big leap of faith in such troubled times, it all made perfect theoretical business sense.

So, in January 2009, while a lot of other companies were floundering or closing their doors, and just three months after Lehman Brothers' spectacular collapse, we officially merged and became 'DKM Blue.'

In all, it probably took six months for us to find and refurbish a new property and then settle everyone into the new regime. Overall, I think it was pretty quick, and being brothers, meant we knew each other's personality which helped enormously. It was also fortunate because dawdling at a time like that would have been very dangerous.

Remarkably, we didn't lose a single client from our former portfolios, but we did lose some staff; some because they became superfluous to needs and others because they didn't like the new management structure.

But the net result was that we reduced our overall staff complement by just over 30% and our general overheads by nearly 50%.

Creating efficiencies such as these has always excited me. Even today I ask myself, 'How do I achieve the optimum streamlined business?' I am always looking at balancing staff numbers against turnover and overheads. That is, I believe, what a good CEO or MD must be able to do.

We also had a significant shift in the way we run our systems. Danny and I looked at how things were done in each business and took the best from both companies. So, while everyone needed to adapt to changing systems, in the end, I don't think there was a massive cultural change for us or the staff.

DKM was essentially a small business in terms of the number of staff, but we had a very positive cash flow, which was achieved by a very flat management system. I believe multi-layered management creates organisational slack and you spend more and more time in meetings than getting the job done.

DK Blue, on the other hand, had quite a large number of staff and significant funds tied up in technology and stock. Also, its management system was a lot more hierarchical.

My preference has always been for a tight team and an open-door policy. I find I get more understanding about staff issues and staff problems running the business that way.

Also, I've always worked 'in the trenches' of the business which helps me know when to jump in and work with my team to keep things going. But I also know when to pull back and take a more holistic view of the operations, and then look for expansion and growth.

I believe those are some of the key things a good leader has to have and enables a real understanding of all aspects of their business, especially when companies are in their formative years.

Being hands-on, running a tight operation and understanding the roles in the business are vital, especially for smaller businesses. Even in a corporation the size of Walmart (2.1 million employees), it is still possible to understand all the various roles within it even you don't actually know them first-hand.

For example, the former CEO of McDonald's, Fred Turner, started out cooking burgers when the company had only 34 employees. He worked his way up and by the time he retired the company had expanded into 118 countries and had over 31,000 outlets. Similarly, media moguls, Barry Diller (net worth US$2.5 billion) and David Geffen (net worth US$6.9 billion), both started out in the mailroom of the William Morris Agency.

So, it is not as uncommon as many people think for successful CEOs to have worked from the ground up. And I believe they are usually the best CEOs because they have that hands-on experience. I also believe they are respected more by their peers and their staff because they have done the hard yards.

Naturally, I am often asked, "How do you handle working with family?"

Obviously, as with 99% of sibling relationships, it is not always easy. I think in some ways it's harder to be in business with a family member than a non-family member because it's often more difficult to be detached from certain issues if they concern a family member.

As you'll remember, Danny and I had already worked together some years before in another company that was owned by our cousin. But we were younger then, so we clashed quite a lot, especially as I was very much thought of as the 'younger brother.'

However, by the time we merged, I was 36 years old, and Danny was 39, so we benefitted from being a lot more mature. We had also become more business educated and articulate with each other.

Of course, we still had arguments and still do, but both of us are more tactful now, and not as hot-headed as when we were younger.

With family, it is natural that there is an emotional element; it would be slightly odd if there wasn't. But I believe I am now pretty good at leaving that aside during business hours.

I believe that a lack of emotional detachment is why a lot of family companies fail, as they make the mistake of treating the business as an extension of the family.

The ones that prosper are, invariably, the ones that respect business and family as separate entities and understand the need for the separation of roles and responsibilities within the company. These families focus on what they need to do to make the business succeed. A partnership with a stranger might also be easier because you can be straight with them. There is no emotional attachment. But if one of you decides to go for a little emotional blackmail there will be an issue, and one of you will get hurt. You must leave family aside and look at issues from a strictly business perspective. If you can confine your discussions to the business at hand, you will be fine.

Our biggest problem was sorting out who did what and who got the final say on certain things; though I believe that was more to do with each of us having years running our own shows rather than sibling rivalry. It was also exacerbated by the fact that when we first founded DKM Blue, Danny and I were joint CEOs. Each of us was just so used to making all the decisions every day we tended to forget about task allocation.

Looking back on the episode, it was no surprise that our two strong personalities clashed again. But with hindsight, I believe we both now understand much of that was probably just ego on both our parts.

But in a business, especially a smaller one you don't always have time to ask for permission to do something. What you need is the freedom to exercise those decisions.

Eventually, the decision was made to bring in an independent arbiter. Harry Cousens, who had also been a part-owner of the Sydney Kings and had become a longtime friend. It was Harry to whom I turned, because of his incredible business acumen. I felt he was the person to help in bring perspective to something Danny and I could not.

Harry was great; he has known us both for a long time but was neither family nor involved in the business.

Moreover, he was very informal in his approach. No endless meetings and long-winded reports, just good old-fashioned advice and straight talking. Not only did his advice clear up most of the differences, it also saved a lot of time.

Harry made us realise that only one person should be entrusted with the role of overseeing the general operations of the business. That should be the CEO or the Managing Director.

So, we both gave up the title of Joint CEO, and I became Managing Director. Although we are equal shareholders, we had to separate that from our management commitments. Most decisions didn't need both our inputs, especially the day-to-day ones.

It is important to understand that a shareholding in and the running of a company are often quite different.

Ultimately, the merger was a good business decision. Within 12 months we had grown turnover by 55% which is pretty impressive in any circumstances, but given the general economic gloom of the time, I think it was remarkable.

With what we now realise were quite trivial matters resolved, we could concentrate on building on our solid foundations and good structure. The company was settled and doing well. It was time to start looking at expansion and diversification.

Of course, family businesses are not only about partnerships as I also have my other brother and my sister working for me. But maintaining the same reasoning of keeping business and family separate, I treat them as I do any other employee. In fact, I believe we are all employed by one company and each of us has a different role with a distinct job description, but we all have a joint responsibility to the company.

It just so happens that my title is Managing Director and my role is to run the company to the best of my abilities. But I hope I am mature enough to know that if there were to come a time when I believed I was not doing that properly or could not do it all, then I would have sufficient self-awareness and courage to step down and appoint someone in my place.

Entrepreneurial Strategies — Chapter Eleven

So, the main lessons we've learnt in merging the companies are:

- Treat everyone as an employee (including yourself!)

- Keep your identity

- Share the same vision.

Treat everyone as an employee (including yourself!)

It doesn't matter whether you are in a family business, partnership or you are an owner operator, the most important thing is to treat the business as a separate entity.

It's not healthy or productive if the two get too intertwined. It can even be destructive.

And you need to keep self-perspective. We are all talented at something, but most of us are not geniuses. As the German philosopher, Arthur Schopenhauer, said, "Talent hits a target no one else can hit. Genius hits a target no one else can see."

I always tell people I mentor: "Don't be afraid to admit you are not a genius because very few people are. So, if you can't do something, just ask for help. Then you will know what to do next time."

Remember not being able to do something and needing help can be the same thing. Don't be too proud. If you really can't cope, it is up to you to put your hand up and admit it. Otherwise, you are failing the business.

You also need to treat every member of the business the same — whether they are family or not. If you give preferential treatment to your family, then the other staff are going to resent them and you. This will have a big impact on morale — so avoid it at all costs.

Giving preferential treatment to your family can also lead them to take advantage of you and not act in the best interests of the business.

At work, I treat my younger brother and sister the same as I do other staff. If they need help personally, then I help them outside of work, not as part of their employment.

One of the impacts of working with family is that as we spend a lot of time together during the week, so once we are outside the office, we tend to enjoy a bit more time apart at weekends. But we still get together at family functions, and when we do we definitely don't talk business.

Keep your identity

Danny and I both have our own identities; I'm more of a flamboyant entrepreneur, whereas he is more conservative in a personal sense. However, those differences can and should be harnessed, and are often very productive when they are. I believe Danny and I now do that successfully.

Building a company is much like building a house. First, comes laying the foundation. Once you have done this, there is a uniform solidity but little identity or aesthetic.

You need to let your identities (the aesthetics) come to the fore slowly within a partnership just as if they were the columns and pediments of the house which grow from its foundations. If you are too strident or domineering, it will lead to discord and, at times, lasting damage. The building may not only fail to grow; it could collapse completely. Get it right though, and you may well find you have built a palace.

You are part a group now, but that does not mean that you can't be an individual. Being an individual is healthy. Just remember a partnership needs balance.

This issue of suppressing or losing our identities was one Danny and I struggled with at the beginning of the partnership. At times, I felt that I was suppressing my identity just to please Danny. No doubt he felt the same. Harry Cousens' arbitration helped us greatly with resolving that problem.

Danny and I compromised, but without losing our individual identities; we are both too strong-willed for that. I realised I couldn't entirely change my nature; it just wasn't possible. Besides that very nature is why I am where I am today.

I also know I can be quite autocratic at times, but when I am it is first and foremost for the sake of the business.

So, although we are an equal partnership, I am the overall head of the company. I think agreeing to that may have been hard for Danny at first, but I have a very clear vision for the company and won't change it. Businesses need clarity of purpose, and I firmly believe that it is my job to deliver on that purpose. Looking at our growth over the years, I can say without false modesty that I have done that.

Share the same vision

Here are a few basic points about a shared vision:

1. Trust should always be mutual and come foremost in a partnership, be it family or otherwise.

2. Make sure that your philosophies are aligned.

3. Have a shared vision for the business. A shared vision is vital, as it brings clarity.

A shared vision is something Danny and I believe in and have achieved. We have always felt growing the business comes first. You need to discuss where you want to be in the next five to ten years. It is what has driven our success in the years since the merger. If we hadn't shared the same vision and values, it would have been a disaster.

What do you both want for the business? If you can't agree then you will destroy the business. We are very fortunate in that we are in line with where DKM Blue is going.

Ultimately, setting up and running a business with someone is like a marriage. You need to talk about the big issues, like whether or not to have children and how you believe they should be brought up. You can't decide any of those things by yourself.

If you don't have a shared vision there will come the point when you realise one, or both of you, are heading in entirely the wrong direction. And when that happens your dreams will fall apart.

Notes

Chapter 12

Acquisitions — Seeing the Possibilities — Planned Growth

Success brings many things. High amongst which are risk, opportunity and potential fulfilment. Maturity also brings many things, the most important of which is, in my opinion, patience. Patience in turn allows you sift the good from the bad and make informed decisions not rash ones. And interestingly it helps you not become complacent.

Of course success can be a key factor in becoming complacent. Making a lot of money allows you to just sit back and enjoy the good life if you want. Worse complacency can lead to a dangerous and destructive level of heightened self-belief. Recent history is littered with tales of people who thought themselves so successful that they could simply do as they please. Of course, as I have mentioned earlier, I had an insight into this sort of behaviour in field of sport when I was just a teenager. As I became successful, I saw it reach much different and disturbing levels.

Remember my motto, learn from other people's mistakes not your own. I was determined that wasn't going to happen to me.

After Danny and me merged we spent the next two to three years stabilising DKM Blue and were rewarded with solid growth during that time.

It was during that period that my mind again turned to expansion through acquisition, but I didn't see anything suitable for quite some time.

Then in 2013, I met Frank Chahoud at a function in Sydney. Frank was the co-founder of one of Australia's oldest and most revered clothing companies, Ambassador Clothing. Although no longer active in the business, he retained a keen interest in it from a personal perspective as his sons, Lawrence and Matthew, were by then running it. Frank suggested I speak to Lawrence and offered to make an introduction.

I felt there could be some synergies that could be exploited as Ambassador Clothing was still producing garments in its Sydney factory so I knew this would mean an expensive product. Surely this was an opportunity for me to offer my Chinese manufacturing facilities and supply to them?

Established in 1944, Ambassador Clothing had a long history in retail. They had manufactured for many high-end labels such as Country Road and, the now sadly gone Marcs brand. They also had their own, very successful, fashion brands Zambelli and Nic Green, which sold in David Jones, Myer and their own chain of fifteen Zambelli stores. Additionally Ambassador had a very impressive portfolio and strong history of government clothing contracts, including one for the NSW Police that ran for more than twenty years.

But no matter how strong a history they had, this was a very difficult time for Australian clothing manufacturing with domestic costs being between a whopping 400% and 700% higher than their offshore counterparts.

In short, clothing manufacturing along with a lot of other sectors was going through an appalling time. Mitsubishi had closed its Australian manufacturing plant five years before and while Lawrence and I were chatting Ford was preparing to shut down its operations here as well. Holden and Toyota would follow suit a year later.

Then in 2013, Australian clothing giant, Pacific Brands, makers of nationally iconic brands such as Bonds and King Gee, signalled the beginning of the end for domestic clothing manufacture when it laid off 1850 staff and moved production offshore.

At the other end of the scale, even small specialist manufacturers such as Winsome Hosiery, with just 14 staff threw in the towel and closed its doors after thirty-five years. But Ambassador Clothing was still struggling to manufacture in Australia, at one point employing over 100 staff.

It was during the meeting with Lawrence, that I thought I could become their offshore supplier and manufacture his company's corporate clothing. However, as we talked, I came to realise that there were other, significant issues that were threatening the business. Overheads and general costs were far too high, and these would eventually drive the company into administration.

Though Lawrence and I kept in contact and became friends, we never discussed the possibility of my buying the company.

Some time later, Ambassador Clothing was pitching for a very lucrative government contract and, in the hope of a big return, this had attracted another friend of Lawrence as an investor. However, when they were unsuccessful in securing the contract, the friend became disenchanted and wanted to divest his interest in the company as quickly as possible. It was then that Lawrence decided to call me with a view to my taking a major stake in the company.

What happened to their business was simply part of the collateral damage suffered by an entire section of Australian industry. They had failed to adapt to a quickly changing business landscape. But neither that nor the loss of the potentially big contract deterred me.

I knew I could turn Ambassador Clothing around by using my existing business model, staff, and premises. I had an excellent setup in China, which could immediately make their whole operation more profitable. In short, I proposed bringing their entire business, with the exception of manufacturing, under the DKM Blue umbrella.

In return, Ambassador would provide DKM Blue with a well-established brand and open doors to a rich history of government contracts. I could see very similar synergies to those that Danny and I had already proved worked very well. I possessed the perfect infrastructure that the company needed to be turned around. For the moment, I had no particular interest in their fashion brands as far as retail was concerned. But I could see their value when offered to corporate clients as a premium designer item. This would also give us a distinct point of difference to other corporate clothing customers.

However, what was paramount for me was that Lawrence and Matthew could make the switch from being bosses to being employees and behaving accordingly. Psychologically, that can be very difficult for some people. If they couldn't, then it would have been a major problem for the company. But more importantly for me was if they left I would lose a lot of their know-how and contacts. Fortunately, they made the transition with ease.

Under the new model, we turned the business into a cash positive venture that allowed us to capitalise on Ambassador Clothing's rich history. Of course, with any change to our business, there were teething issues such as having our staff and cultures adapt. This is normal, but if we hadn't had staff buy-in to our vision and strategy this acquisition would not have worked.

I also looked very closely at Ambassador's client ledger. Being an old established company there was a large number of customers listed, but I cut out all the dead wood. Some had been inactive for a few years and some were bad payers. I trimmed everything back to only working with the customers in which I could see a profitable future.

Toward the end of their former incarnation, Ambassador Clothing essentially concentrated on the corporate side of their business and closed the retail fashion division. Their decision was based not only on the high cost of domestic manufacturing and soaring retail rents but the ferocious competition that was coming from international brands such as Zara, Uniqlo and Topshop which were now dominating both the 'bricks and mortar' and online landscapes alike. The cumulative result of all these negatives was that by the time I brought it under the DKM Blue umbrella, the company had been bleeding money to the tune of minus 48% EBIT. Bluntly, they were losing forty-eight cents for every dollar they turned over. However, the deal I eventually struck allowed me to obtain a company that was completely unencumbered by debt as well as reducing the staffing overhead by 98% which essentially meant just Lawrence and Matthew joined the new operation while all other functions were distributed throughout the existing DKM Blue infrastructure.

Then two years later my second acquisition opportunity came about just as unexpectedly.

It started during Mercedes-Benz Fashion Week when I met Kevin Weldon at an after-show event. This meeting highlights the power of networking if you do it properly. Kevin, a prominent Australian entrepreneur and spritely octogenarian, is a recipient of The Order of Australia with a highly-respected background in publishing. I am pleased to say that we have a very good professional acquaintance now but back then as we chatted, he mentioned that one of his goddaughters ran a successful women's fashion business that he had profitably invested in at one point. He also thought she and I should meet as there could be some mutually advantageous opportunities.

Women's fashion is fast moving, emotive and above all, a high-risk business, which like the music industry is littered with more failures than successes.

So, despite the acquisition of Ambassador Clothing, I explained to Kevin that women's fashion was not an area in which I was interested. But as a courtesy, I gave him my card and the meeting slipped into the back of my mind.

However, one of Kevin's great qualities is his curiosity. It was this that led him to email me a few weeks later and ask if he could come and see what I did.

This was refreshing for me since I get a lot of calls asking for help and advice but not so many from people simply because they are interested in what I do. He was both interested and impressed by my operation. I, in turn, liked him and admired his success and continued interest in the business world, especially at an age when most would have retired. After that, we kept in touch.

It was about three months after our initial meeting that Kevin mentioned to me that his goddaughter's company, which had over 20 fashion labels was suddenly, like every Australian clothing company, struggling against the influx of foreign megabrands and had, as a result, entered into administration.

The story was by now a sad but familiar one to me. There was nothing wrong with the brands but they were facing extinction nonetheless. Kevin, however, felt that the way I had so successfully streamlined Ambassador Clothing would work in this situation too. Sure, there were differences in end product and marketing, but essentially it was a management and supply chain issue at heart.

In his opinion, I was someone with the talent and track record to overcome both of these obstacles and put the company back on its feet. Despite his assurances, I was still reticent because of the higher risk factor. Eventually, I agreed to set up a meeting to see if anything could be done to help.

Chapter 12 Acquisitions — Seeing the Possibilities — Planned Growth

One of the things that excited me was the strength of the company had built with boutique manufacturers in China. This was the factor that changed my mind because I could immediately see the broader benefits for my company as a whole.

At the time, most Chinese factories needed a basic minimum of 500 pieces per style because their production was primarily geared up for Europe and America. Of course, this meant their prices were very competitive, but at the same time, the combined populations of Europe and the USA exceeded 1.3 billion people whereas Australia's was a mere 23 million.

European and American companies can place opening orders of tens of thousands of units in a single style and easily repeat that three or four times per season. Furthermore, they have much bigger ranges than Australian labels.

During the time I am referring to, for example, Spanish monolith Zara's Chinese manufacturers produced some 450 million garments for them in a single a year. That's over 1.2 million garments a day!

The effect of all this is not so much that Chinese factories won't make what they consider a small order for Australia, but you run the risk of being bumped down the waiting list if something bigger and better comes their way. I completely understand their point of view, but it can put a domestic label in a very perilous position. So, finding good, small-run factories is always difficult for Australian labels. Here was an opportunity to access a valuable manufacturing pool.

I adhere to the dictum that a thing is sweeter if free, and essentially, I was receiving a free piece of infrastructure that could enhance my company's overall product offer.

But, again at the heart of the matter, was the potential synthesis of talents, infrastructure, and finance that appealed and would produce a return to fortune for this floundering company as well as a broadening of customer base and increase in group profits for me.

Additionally, I sensed this opportunity would provide me with the means to re-launch Ambassador Clothing's fashion labels onto the retail market. I believed it would solve the David-and-Goliath syndrome Zambelli would face during the early stages of fighting for a small share of a market when it risked becoming quickly dominated by multinational giants.

But I still exercised caution when completing the deal and bought what was left of the company at that point from the administrator plus just the three of the labels I felt still had potential plus the exclusive distribution rights for three well-renowned European labels.

Again, it was important to me to have the key personnel come on board as part of the purchase. Essentially, we just brought across the Creative Director, thereby reducing the staff by twenty people. I christened the new fashion subsidiary, DKM Blue Management.

Chapter 12 Acquisitions — Seeing the Possibilities — Planned Growth

Once again, I bought a debt free company and significantly reduced staff. This time by 99.5%!

By now I could also see a marked reversal of fortune for Ambassador Apparel as it was now rechristened, with EBIT returning to 22% positive. To put that in perspective, I had improved the overall pre-tax earnings by 66% in just two years and felt the time and circumstances were right for speculation on a further phase for their fashion brands. I was correct, and shortly after, I set about re-launching Ambassador's dormant Zambelli brand by utilising the newly acquired manufacturing pool, which, as far as I know, was the first major re-launch of its kind in the Australian fashion industry.

I relish challenges in which the odds are stacked against me. So, this was something I really wanted to embrace. Moving the production to China was relatively easy, but getting the finished product exactly right took a lot more time and fine-tuning. However, I remained patient and had a very soft initial launch.

To make high-quality men's shirts in what was essentially a dress factory, I introduced new training schemes and systems, and equipped it with several pieces of new, specialist equipment. The new equipment had a trifold benefit. It displayed my commitment, produced a superior product and gave me greater control in the production without any real investment.

I now had the time to concentrate on phase two which was to take the business online with Zambelli.com.au. This would be another first for the brand. I synchronised this launch with that of a flagship retail outlet in Sydney's Balmain and followed up some months later with both men's and women's wholesale collections for Australia and New Zealand.

Neither of the companies I became involved in would have survived without my intervention, so I am glad I have been able to help two important Australian clothing companies stay viable.

I believe the Australian fashion industry was a very bleak place for standalone, domestic companies, especially if they had no export market. Because of this environment, I think it would have been quite foolhardy to try and launch an independent Australian fashion label then. Though obviously, that is a great shame because there is a lot of talent here, but nearly all of it, much like that in the music and acting fraternities is forced to go overseas to make a decent living.

I suppose all that I have written about domestic fashion manufacturing and retailing is why numerous people have said I was mad to get involved, but I have always bucked trends. So yes, I was going into a business that was risky, but I had mitigated those risks and reduced costs to a point where I was totally in control. Where a blip in the market would have sunk a traditional fashion company, it wouldn't harm me in the least.

The key to all businesses, of whatever type, is cost control. Naturally, there are numerous ways in which cost control can be managed. I will discuss those methods in greater detail in the following chapter. My theory, which has fortunately worked extremely well for me is that, right from the very start of my career, I have always had my own very successful, centralised sourcing and quality control office in Shanghai. This is DKM Blue's major competitive advantage but not its only one.

By bringing DKM Blue's new fashion brands together, I also reduced a host of backend costs and simultaneously increased joint buying power. This makes each brand a simple cost centre that is managed by the corporate umbrella I control.

In this manner, I managed to reduce the overall operating costs of all the fashion and corporate clothing subsidiaries by approximately AUS$5 million. Now those divisions are lean, slick and in a position to stand up against the global giants in a manner that would have been unthinkable in their previous incarnations.

I am proud to say that in womenswear alone my brands are stocked in more than 350 independent retailers across Australia and New Zealand.

I also absorbed another Australian womenswear brand, Mint. Its look is somewhat different to the other brands and therefore complements rather than conflicts with them.

Of course, there was still mayhem in the marketplace as standalones succumbed to the pressures and either shut their doors or went under. But who was to replace them? My current stable did not cover sufficient looks.

The Disruption Theory is well known in economics but equally well served with the phrase coined by the Ancient Roman philosopher, Lucretius, more than two thousand years ago. Roughly translated it is, 'One man's meat is another man's poison.'

Enter Silique.

Silique is a women's fashion brand created entirely within DKM Blue.

What is more, it was brought to the market in just three months. The brilliant part for me was that because it was created in-house it cost extremely little. We did everything ourselves from creating the name, designing the ranges and labelling right through to the photography. Even the range samples were made by our existing manufacturers. As all orders are indent, there is not even any stock risk. That's my kind of business!

Essentially, I have taken the course of ignoring the global giants, as I am not yet ready to go head to head with them. They can have their market, and I intend, for the moment to concentrate on mine. It's all about niche targeting and growth control.

Chapter 12   Acquisitions — Seeing the Possibilities — Planned Growth

Now that we have a multi-brand, consolidated sourcing model, I can get runs of as few as fifty garments per design at very reasonable prices due to the overall volume I place. That would be totally impossible if I was a standalone.

I have always maintained it is much better to work smarter, not harder. By offering my clients a range of products, their operating costs, such as freight consolidation, etc. are considerably reduced too.

I believe DKM Blue is now unique in its spread of product lines, which includes: merchandise, corporate clothing, fashion, and accessories. None of our competitors come even close!

All of this has meant that the last four years have been a steep learning curve for everyone at DKM Blue, including me. As far as my staff are concerned, I have worked hard to alleviate the effects of all these changes. So, while they are working with more product lines and types, staff members still retain the same hours.

To achieve the changes without too much disruption, I did restructure certain people's roles, particularly in production. Previously each person was responsible for particular brands and lines, but at times found themselves not as busy as their co-workers. The change was very simple, all work is now pooled and tasks rather than brands allocated to each individual. It is much more efficient. Accounting, warehousing, and logistics are all centralised with the only exception being sales staff that remain in their specialised areas of the business. It is still a matter of product in and product out.

Of course, it is also essential that existing customers aren't affected or feel neglected during times of change. You need to work very hard at preventing that. They should simply enjoy the benefits of having greater choice. Again, I believe we have all pulled together and managed the changes and challenges that confronted us.

Ambassador and DKM Management benefitted from the commitment and support of considerable resources, both fiscal and managerial.

However my next acquisition was a lot more to do with mentoring and helping someone achieve their entrepreneurial dreams than hard cash.

For me success and maturity are also about remembering my own humble beginnings and putting myself back in the shoes of my twenties, when I was struggling to make a few hundred bucks here and there.

So I have for many years now acted as a mentor to numerous would-be entrepreneurs and this has recently culminated with me working as an ambassador for Chivas Regal's The Venture, an initiative that rewards businesses who want to generate positive change.

The Oxford dictionary defines the word mentor as 'An experienced and trusted advisor'.

The advice and knowledge of a talented and experienced entrepreneur who has already made the difficult climb themselves can help ease the burden of beginners reaching their own peak. Climbing it requires a marathon effort and having a mentor guiding the would-be entrepreneur helps them endure until they reach the top. Moreover, this mentoring trains them how to stay on top of the mountain.

So when I became involved with Chivas Regal's 'The Venture' I was well prepared for sifting the good from the bad.

Furthermore I saw it as chance to explore and help one or more fledgling entrepreneur achieve their dreams.

Sitting in the crowd of the Australian finals and watching companies deliver their five minute pitch to establish why they should represent Australia in the finals in New York, Tom Lawrence's 2013 start-up, Swanky Socks, really stood out for me.

Even though Tom did not win the overall competition, I admired what he had done in just four years and how he created his own opportunity by entering The Venture.

Not long after listening to him and subsequently meeting with him, I decided to take a 50% stake in his start up.

Here was a product that would be constantly in demand around the world via an e-commerce platform. A product both functional and fashionable that required little in the way of investment or warehousing yet had the potential to return a healthy profit all year round.

Moreover it met all my self-imposed criteria for a synergistic fit with DKM Global.

To reiterate these are.

- Physically fit within our Head Office complex

- Utilise existing infrastructure of e-commerce design & management, logistics and accounting etc.

- No staff other than company principal to be brought over

- Strategic management by me

- A strong possibility of crossing over to corporate clients and enhancing our existing offer in this arena

- A comfortable fit with the other fashion brands I control

But above all, Tom is young and ambitious, just like me when I started out, so I have a natural affinity with him and want to help him succeed and I now have the time and money to treat Swanky Socks as a long term investment.

As I have matured as an entrepreneur and person, I have come to realise that opportunities come along all the time. Of course I have always known not to grab all opportunities whether they are good or bad, but I did, when younger and less mature, sometimes wonder whether they would continue come or if they were more akin to luck and the winning streak might run out.

Let me assure you they do not.

Entrepreneurial Strategies — Chapter 12

Here is a brief summary of what I've learnt from our acquisitions:

- Discard what doesn't work.

- Look at your systems; are they maximised to full capacity?

- Look at your customer list; are they all active? If you can't reactivate them, they're not clients.

- Keep key staff: Make sure you perform regular staff reviews. As well as your view of their performance, what are the individual's ambitions? Can you accommodate them?

- Respect the company's heritage: If you acquire a company, it is fine to make it more efficient, but don't destroy what it is known for. Make sure you understand the underlying mechanics of what you have bought.

- Have clearly-defined roles: Your existing staff should already have defined roles, but when people from an acquired company come on board, it is particularly important to clearly define their roles, especially if they have previously been a principal or director who has been used to running their own show.

Notes

Chapter 13

Running a Successful Company – Bottom Line – Profit Over Turnover

'To succeed in business, to reach the top, an individual must know all it is possible to know about that business.'
— J. Paul Getty

Running a business is a big responsibility. You are responsible for yourself, your clients, suppliers, and staff. I knew when I founded my company that I had begun something that would impact on my life, as well as others. And that impact might be good or bad. Naturally, I wanted it to be good for everyone.

I also realised that when my customers spent money with me, I would spend money with my suppliers and stimulate their businesses. When they spend, it does the same and so on. It's often referred to as the 'Ripple Effect.' Obviously not spending (when times are tough) has the opposite effect. This is what creates peaks and troughs and the smaller the company the more these affect it.

That is why I always concentrate on profitability, not turnover. Turnover is money on paper; profit is real money. You should always bear this in mind because most small businesses are financed by borrowing or run on a shoestring, and only profit will keep them going.

You would be amazed how many people, especially those starting out in business, ask me what my turnover over is and how many people I employ.

Socially it is, of course, extremely rude, but more importantly, it displays a distinct lack of business acumen. As I have written before, the success of a company is about balancing income and costs to maximise profits.

Remember: turnover has nothing to do with profit, nor do staff levels. You could, on paper, be achieving a gross margin of 50% but if your overheads are too high it will be seriously eroded!

Calculating your margins is a real skill and needs to be done with care. Take into account every cost you have as a percentage of the total cost on which you calculate your margin not just the unit production of the item. One of your biggest variable costs will be salary — yours included.

A lot of people think that by increasing their turnover, they are getting richer, but that doesn't take into account the higher risk involved (the original investment) and the smaller return on investment.

I would rather turn over a million dollars with a 40% margin than two million with only 20% margin. Why? Because I end up with the same amount of gross profit (profit before overheads). So why should I have double the risk, worry and work for the same amount of money?

Protect what you work for.

Remember my key mantra, "Work smarter not harder."

I have never believed that all my customers will be with me for life. That is not to say my company doesn't have a lot of loyal customers or that I don't work hard to keep them, I do. My record of service and reliability has created longevity with them. But I am realistic enough to understand that they are driven by the bottom line too. Despite that, I have proved by offering good service and reliability that customer retention is something which is possible to achieve consistently.

Think of the marketplace as a pie. Your job is to get the biggest piece of it (market share). And don't expect market share to fall into your lap. It won't; you have to work for it.

So always make sure you spend a regular amount of your time marketing and selling, even if you don't like it!

Marketing and selling are two completely separate disciplines that most companies and people confuse. Even the typical title of 'Sales & Marketing Manager' has the functions the wrong way round.

Marketing is letting people know who you are and what you do. It's about stimulating opportunities. Selling is converting these opportunities into solid sales that deliver profits.

I am always aware that when I get a new sale, it means I have taken it from someone else. And I also always remember the same thing can happen to me. So always be prepared because no one has a monopoly in the marketplace.

Of course, if you are very talented or very lucky you may have a unique product that offers a virgin marketing opportunity. Then you can monopolise the world with your product or service. But that rarely happens.

As an example, take something we all use like mobile phones. When they first appeared on the market, they were unique. Just having them to sell guaranteed you a good living because demand outstripped supply. Now, however, it's a different story.

So, acknowledge you have competitors and keep thinking about finding new ways of increasing your market share. Do this, and you won't go far wrong.

Another great marketing tool I recommend is referrals. Referrals are invaluable and a good way to stimulate interest in your company. Referrals will only come if you have a demonstrable history of good service, reliability, and longevity.

Because my company has such a history, I have gained a lot of business through referrals.

But if you or your company does not get a lot of referrals it may be worth asking your existing customers to refer you to someone they know. I have found that most of my customers are flattered when I have asked them for a recommendation. It shows I value them. The best thing about this way of gaining new customers is that it costs you absolutely nothing in real dollar terms.

By using this method to stimulate opportunities you have controlled your overall costs and time in order to invest in marketing and stimulate sales. And I used the word 'stimulate' not 'create' deliberately. Far too often I hear people talking about 'creating sales.' They aren't. They have just increased their market share — the market didn't get bigger, just their share of it did.

Running a tight ship is also a powerful marketing tool. It shows your customers and staff that you know what you are doing. I have also found that some people think 'running a tight ship' is just having a load of strict and pointless rules, particularly in smaller companies. That's not it at all. Running a tight ship is about integrating a whole range of disciplines to produce an efficient whole. Let's examine cost cutting as one of those.

Do you believe you could cut the cost of running your business by 1%?

Of course, you do!

Now imagine you could identify ten different operations in your business and save 1% in each? That would give you a total cost saving of 10%.

Let's suppose you are turning over a half million dollars a year. Adding up all your 1% savings would be $50,000 in pure profit! Wouldn't you like that?

Customers like to know you are controlling your costs because it shows them you are careful with their money!

You might ask, "Whose money?" You've earned it, so why can't you spend it as you please? Well, if your customers see you (with your half million turnover) driving a customised Maserati and taking expensive three-hour lunches every day, they might just wonder if you are charging them too much, or if you are just having fun and not paying attention to running your company properly.

I enjoy my success, but I control my personal spending too.

Being careful and only spending what I can afford is something I have done from the very start and will always do. I have worked too hard to squander what I have earned.

Cutting costs is easy. For instance, if we stick with the phone example, you can always get a better deal on your cell phone plan because now the providers are fighting for your piece of the pie (See what I mean about not expecting customers for life?).

But what's involved? Is the new service as good? Are there 'hidden' costs? How much hassle will be involved in the actual changeover? Distraction takes away your time. So, always remember Benjamin Franklin's advice — time is money.

I think a smarter answer would be to look at how you use your phone — then that is making cost control work for you.

Suppose you decided to send a hundred texts a day instead of making a hundred calls? Not only would you save money, but you would also save time (you could spend an allotted part of your day replying to texts rather than answering every call as it comes in).

Making decisions in business is very easy. Consistently making good decisions is hard, but good entrepreneurs have to be able to do this all the time. And knowing and acknowledging you are wrong is often a hard lesson to learn, particularly when you are the boss.

I understand being the boss places me not only in a position of power but responsibility too.

Remember this when you are offered advice. Your position of power allows you to dismiss opinion and dominate any conversation. But is that good management? Of course, as the head of the company the decision is ultimately yours. But a smart operator listens to what people have to say and then decides. It may be good or bad advice, but it costs nothing to listen. I have learned being a good listener is smart. That's how you learn in business and life.

And don't only question others' advice, question your own. Think things through from more than one angle. Consider cause and effect.

Isaac Newton wrote: "To every action, there is an equal and opposite reaction."

That is why I always think things through before making a decision. You don't have to spend ages; it's just like sport or chess. If I do this, what is the likely outcome? As I said earlier I never just 'shoot from the hip.'

I find now I don't need to consciously 'think' about decisions as they've become instinctive, but just as measured. And remember, no one is perfect. It is good to strive for perfection, but often 'good' will suffice. Particularly if it delivers a product or service at best cost/benefit ratio to your client, hasn't induced massive stress and, most importantly, produced a healthy profit for you.

I am a firm believer that everything happens for a reason and always look for the positives in all situations. It is because of this that I have come to accept that even bad outcomes can potentially produce good results.

Starting your own company and making it successful involves hard work. Lots of hard work! So, does learning how to make good decisions, which is an essential part of working smarter, not harder.

Not everyone likes hard work though. For instance, I have interviewed a lot of Gen Ys and Millennials and found they have different ideas about hard work. They look at huge multinationals and think every company should have breakout areas and amenities like gyms and bars. But small companies just can't afford those sorts of things.

In a big company, the cost of installing a gym is negligible when spread across a large number of staff. But if you employ three or four staff it is just not going to work.

If I interview someone with that sort of attitude, I don't hire them. What I look for are people who want to learn from me.

In my early days, I had to teach myself to do a lot of things. So, I worked hardest at the things I wasn't as good at or didn't enjoy because they were my weak links and a chain is only as strong as its weakest link.

Technology has helped us immensely with certain tasks, but it has also made the world a small place. Think about book and music stores. Technology destroyed the traditional aspects of these two industries by exploiting their weak links; internet sales wiping out the first and downloads the second.

These days, entrepreneurs will be fighting multinationals from day one. There are boundless stories of entrepreneurs at first failing before succeeding, but I don't believe that it is necessary to fail to eventually find success. Failure is going out of business; lack of success is not having enough business, which is where perseverance and intuition come in. I had to teach myself not to listen to my negative thoughts because that is when you will have a lot of time to fear 'fear' itself. It was one of my hardest lessons. But as long as you are convinced that your gut feeling is correct and you understand what you are getting yourself into, you will be ready for success when the work starts to flow.

With experience, you will find it easier to understand the peaks and troughs of business cycles. I have always planned for them, costed them and by doing this was prepared. This is where cost control becomes really important, and so my company is a very good example of this.

Because pre-Christmas is a peak time when most of my customers spend a good part of their half yearly budgets, my company has a trough every January. And a lot of the product we deliver in late December will not be paid for until late January.

So, because there is not much business activity during very late December and early January, I close the company just before Christmas for annual holidays, which includes at least two weeks of January. Essentially that means I have to finance twelve months of my company's activities on about eleven months' income. But, because I have planned for that trough, it doesn't bother me. I, too, can go on holiday and not have to worry.

Learning to run a company is like learning to run a marathon; you will flag at points, need drinks, breaks, etc., but with training and experience, you will not only cross the finish line you will win!

Entrepreneurial Strategies — Chapter Thirteen

These are the main points I'd like you to take away from this chapter:

- Profitability, not turnover

- Getting and keeping customers requires effort

- Smart cost cutting equals pure profit.

Profitability, not turnover

Often people will focus on the 'turnover' figure of a company, rather than focusing on what is the real indicator of a business's success, its profit. For example, someone might boast that their business is consistently turning over $150,000 a month but they might actually have expenses of $145,000 a month leaving a total profit of $5,000.

It is important to drill down on your business figures to work out exactly how much the business makes after all expenses are calculated. I've also seen that some small business owners calculate profit before factoring in their wage. But profit should be calculated at what the business is left with once the owner has paid themselves a decent wage.

Getting and keeping customers requires effort

Customers won't just fall in your lap. Acquiring customers means you are 'taking' those customers from someone else, so you need to work at it. First, those customers need to know that you exist and provide what they want, which is a matter of clever marketing. Once the potential customer knows about you that is when you can begin to sell your product or service to them.

Once you've acquired a new customer, then I believe in a back to the basics approach of good customer service and reliability to keep those customers. By proving your reliability over the long term, those customers can then even be encouraged to refer other potential customers, thus continuing the cycle and growing the customer base further.

Smart cost cutting equals pure profit

With the cost of running a business increasing yearly, it can feel like you are just trying to make more sales, to pay ever increasing bills! However, no matter how profitable your business, there are ways that you can cut costs and increase profits. The most likely places to find cost cutting opportunities are space/rent, telecommunications, utilities and printing. There will probably be potential for 'quick wins' for your business by looking at these areas alone.

Notes

Chapter 14

The Big Picture — The World Now Can Really Be Your Oyster

The Big Picture

Seeing the 'big picture' is akin to seeing a huge, flashing neon sign. Too often, though, blinkered conditioning prevents people from seeing this 'big picture,' and they remain concerned about the small things.

Someone pointed out to me once that if everyone could see what I see, then no one would ever shine above the rest because everyone would be shining. There cannot be leaders without followers, and there will always be followers — no amount of inspiration or education will ever change that. If you are to be a leader, hoping to aspire to great heights, you must prepare yourself psychologically for how your life will change as a result.

You must also be sensible and not get carried away with your newfound wealth by blowing it away on frivolous luxuries or destructive lifestyles, or expanding your business too fast in a desperate attempt to gain every inch you can. If you do, you may find you lose everything you've built up far faster than you acquired it. I've seen too many people rise to success without being mentally equipped for it, only to find they are broke soon after.

There's also, what in Australia we call the 'tall poppy syndrome,' where as soon as you poke your head up, someone, somewhere, will try to chop it off.

Failure can be an important lesson too, but as I said previously it makes sense to avoid it if you can. I'd rather learn my lesson from observing other people's mistakes, than making my own.

I'm not saying I don't make mistakes. Far from it, I've made my fair share. There will always be circumstances you cannot control, but where things that happen around you and to you are within the realm of your control, there is no real excuse for failure. When going into a situation where a risk factor is evident, I plan ahead to minimise any possible negative exposure.

Every successful person has had ups and downs. Preparing for the down times, minor or major, is simply a matter of training one's mind to find the positive in any situation. It's said if someone offers you a lemon make lemonade. Visualisations were once scoffed upon, but this technique is not only widely accepted now but is becoming a standard tool. It costs nothing and is accessible to everyone; you just have to train yourself to do it.

Even if you have a natural aptitude for visualisation, you must still train yourself to do it effectively. Pianists may be born with natural ability, but that does not mean they are automatically at concert-level performance. They must practice, practice, practice, to achieve mastery. And so it is with all aspects of life. The moment you stop learning is the moment you die.

How much has visualisation contributed to my success? It's hard to gauge, but I know one thing for certain — it definitely helped!

When you train yourself to think positively, you have the potential to change not only your life but also the lives of those around you; sometimes without even realising it at the time. By believing in myself, overcoming obstacles and using positive visualisation, I set out on the right path without ever consciously deciding to do so.

It is exciting to see people take that first step to improving themselves. That first step is unquestionably the hardest. And when you see someone doing that, you react naturally by wanting to help him or her because you sense they are eager to learn. The choice is yours. If you don't choose to do it for yourself, no one can make you do it. Choosing to do so, though, and helping others to do so as well, is enormously rewarding.

Things haven't always been rosy for me. In my early 20s, it was tough feeling I wasn't getting anywhere. My first year in business was particularly difficult because there was virtually no income. Being forced to live on very little income at 22, when my friends were earning far more money and could do and buy things that I couldn't was very dispiriting. I had my basketball, which brought me great joy but no income. Even to go out for a drink with my mates was a challenge. I'd make a quick buck here and there, buying something and reselling it, but I feared I would never get ahead. I wondered how I would ever be able to afford a home of my own.

The turning point was changing my way of thinking. Instead of thinking about the money, I began thinking of building the right belief system, building the right model and knowing that the money would come if I focused on finding my niche, my passion.

I am an optimist by nature and fortunately have always believed in myself. But there will always be dark moments, no matter how positive I am. The key to overcoming them is to accept them and move on.

It is how you bounce back from despair that counts. It requires willpower and a 'can do' attitude, something you can build in yourself without any tool other than willingness. Don't be a quitter. Don't be prepared to lose.

If you suffer low self-esteem or don't have strong willpower, and don't try to change, but just keep doing what you've always done, then you'll never achieve anything.

To change your life, you need to change yourself. It is a discipline. Remember how I began by making the conscious decision to make my company appear bigger than it was right from the start? Every day, consciously focus on what is positive in your life. Count your blessings, literally, however, basic they may be. Make a list and reread it when you feel a weak moment coming on. Do you have a roof over your head, food on the table, your health, a loving family and good friends? You might be surprised at how long this list is. And once you've tallied up those blessings, say a thank you for each and every one of them. Do this for a few minutes every day as gratitude lifts your spirits.

I drove a beat-up van to work every morning because that was all I could afford. It wasn't exactly a chick magnet; I was too embarrassed to even to drive it to a club or into the city. Those times make me appreciate the good times.

Success does not protect you from those dark moments. The sun still throws dark shadows on occasion. Sometimes I feel sad that I seem to have few real friends and that those around me may be there for selfish reasons.

When I do, I'll take some time to myself. Alone time helps me. We can't always be on a high; everything doesn't go right all of the time. Life isn't perfect. But there is an advantage in knowing that when we're feeling down it can be a healthy way to re-establish balance. That's what I meant about finding the silver lining, no matter what. If life was a constant high, we would never appreciate the good times. To cherish the highs, you must suffer the lows.

Entrepreneurial Strategies — Chapter Fourteen

Don't grow too big, too quickly

If your business proves to be successful, pat yourself on the back but don't spend your money too quickly. By spending rashly, even if it is on expanding the business, you risk making bad decisions and losing what you've made. Instead, provide yourself with a 'buffer' of profit, so that if your sales the following year are not as strong, you'll be able to ride the downturn without losing everything. Ask yourself whether you want to look flashy now and go bust, or if you want to be successful over the long term. If the answer is the latter, which I would hope it is, then prepare for long-term success with careful spending and expansion.

Positive thinking takes discipline

Visualisation is a wonderful tool, but it only works if you practise it consistently. Training your brain is like training any other muscle and takes practise over the long term to see changes. Taking time out alone can be part of this brain training program, and is something I personally find helpful to rid my mind of clutter and negative self-talk. While some people are probably more positive thinkers than others, there are some easy ways to increase your positivity, which include being grateful. Research has shown that practising being grateful regularly will increase positive thinking.

Focus on values, not money

It's easy to get caught in the trap of focusing on making enough money for the business to survive. However, focusing just on making money will not lead to success or happiness. The way to business success is to focus on building a strong business model based on values that reflect and improve upon the best in your industry. It's a little bit like the Kevin Costner movie, *Field of Dreams*, where Kevin Costner's character hears a voice which says, "Build it, and they will come" except in business it should be "Build it right, and they will come."

Notes

Chapter 15

Life is Amazing! — Enjoying the Fruits Of Your Hard Work

Danish author Karen Blixon once said, "People know that the real glory of dreams lies in their atmosphere of unlimited freedom." And yet so many people do not believe that.

Many years ago, some friends of mine went to see a documentary called *The Secret*, which was based on the book by the same name. It had become something of a phenomenon because it promised to reveal the way to success. I think they assumed I had seen it too because by then I was starting to be quite successful. When I said I hadn't their comeback was, "What? So, things just happen for you?" They thought I was connected to the same cosmic force.

Of course, I wasn't. I was connected to a lot of hard work and determination. But I was a bit curious, so I went along and saw the movie. It didn't provide me with any new insights, just a good laugh because I had already instinctively been doing what it preached for most of my life.

I say this because I want everyone reading this book to realise and believe that there is no 'secret.' If I can do what I have done, anyone can.

Let me give you an example. I had never been a big reader of autobiographies or business books until someone gave me a copy of Richard Branson's 1998 classic, *Losing My Virginity*.

What a revelation! I devoured that book from cover to cover. I was mesmerised. This entrepreneur, famous for his global success and cosmic vision, began his business, his dream, with the same mental approach I had. Despite Branson having more than twenty years' head start, I must admit that my success is hardly at the level of this multi-layered billionaire.

What is the same though is that I began my company based on a business plan scribbled on scraps of paper just like he did. Neither of us had expensive consultants or slick presentations; there were only the handwritten notes of dreams and aspirations penned on bits of paper. So, are we so different?

Some claim you must develop an impressively comprehensive business plan before you can ever get ahead. Frankly, that's bullshit. It is fine to keep it simple. Reading Branson's book reaffirmed that for me.

I still keep my scraps of paper locked safely away. They serve as a reminder of my humble beginnings.

The chances Richard Branson took and how he

manoeuvred things in his favour, and how I have progressed are more similar than they may first appear. While reading his autobiography, I became even more convinced than ever that I had chosen the right path. I was equally convinced that others who did likewise could also achieve the seemingly impossible.

Seeing the big picture means taking a step back, so its size does not swamp you. Too often, though our blinkered conditioning prevents us doing just that and we fail to notice the obvious. Sometimes I have difficulty explaining this. To me, it is so clear, but others can't always see what I'm seeing.

Of course, everyone is not the same; some play instruments, some play sport and so forth. Each takes a particular set of skills, and not everyone has the same skill set.

And so, it is that some cannot instinctively see the big picture. But you have to remember that that is just part of what you need to be successful. Furthermore, it can be learned. Just like music or sport, we may not all be Carlos Santana or Michael Jordan, but with practice, we can learn how to pluck some chords or shoot some hoops.

What I mean by this is to play to your strengths and work on overcoming your weaknesses. A weakness isn't a weakness once you understand how to improve what you are not good at.

One of the ways I have done this, and which I mentioned earlier was to deliberately seek out people who were more successful than me. I spoke to them, observed them and learned what their strengths and weaknesses were.

More importantly, I came to realise they were just like everyone else. They too had their strengths and weaknesses, but what they did have in common was their ability to maximise the effects of their strengths and minimise those of their weaknesses. Sir Richard Branson is, for instance, dyslexic, but has used this condition to his advantage by the simplicity of his management style.

One of my weaknesses that, fortunately, I have come to understand and overcome is being hurt by the way people changed toward me as I became successful. Some were jealous, some envious and others tried to exploit our friendship for their advantage. I am, after all, human. But over time, I came to realise that, for the most part, these emotions were their feelings, not mine. So, I learned to ignore the jealous, tried where I could to help the envious and toughened up with the exploitative.

However, whether you like it or not, you will inevitably lose some friends as you become more successful, either by your choice or theirs. Interestingly, I have spoken to other successful people about this and they all agree it is just 'par for the course.' Knowing and understanding that has helped me.

Of course, we all lose friends and make new ones, but once you have become successful, there is always the well-founded doubt that people may be befriending you for what you have and not who you are.

When I started to reap the rewards of all my hard work, I found I had a lot of new acquaintances, but not many new true friends. I knew it would happen, but it was still hard to accept.

Of course, I hope that these things do not happen to you when you are successful. Perhaps they won't, but as with everything else, if you are prepared for it, then you can handle it.

Other people maintain I changed as I became successful, but I disagree. I'm still intrinsically the same person. It is other people's perceptions of me that have changed. One of the reasons I know that I have not changed is my attitude to money and business. I remained sensible with how I spent my money, and I didn't indulge in self-destructive behaviour, like partying and drugs, because you can't behave that way if you have a business to run.

So, my advice is to stay true to yourself and take your time. Resist the temptation to overspend on yourself or over-expand your business too fast in a desperate attempt to gain every inch you can.

Doing either or both is a sure-fire way to lose everything you've built up far faster than you acquired it. I've seen many people rise to success and then lose the lot because they were not mentally equipped for it.

The media is full of stories about fast-rising celebrities who resort to self-destructive behaviour such as taking drugs and drinking to excess. Perhaps they can't believe they've made it and this is a way of coping.

But these are the symptoms, not the cause. Essentially, it is a lack of preparation for success, and they've failed to stay grounded. They've climbed the mountain but lost their balance. I was lucky in that I had witnessed such behaviour first-hand when I was a teenager mixing with some very successful American basketball players. Often these guys had come from quite poor backgrounds and had no idea of how to cope with sudden wealth. I think in many ways that helped me avoid the same pitfalls.

Of course, some things will always happen that are beyond your control. Being successful won't stop that. But if you are just careless then you have no one to blame but yourself, and making excuses is just lying to yourself.

People need heroes and role models, be they sports or acting stars, musicians or writers. We each like to watch someone win in the field of endeavour we admire and think, *Wow! What must that be like? How did they do it?*

Of course, not everyone on the planet watching the Oscars or the Olympics decides to be an actor or sportsperson. But how many times have you heard someone say during their acceptance speech that they were inspired to do what they did by someone they admired in their chosen field?

So even if our successes are not as stellar as an Oscar or Olympic gold medal, it is still exciting to see people improving themselves and know you have somehow been instrumental in that.

The rocky start to my career made me even more determined to go it alone, to start a company and do things properly, on my own terms.

When I did start my company, visualisation helped me do things properly. I concentrated on picturing not my parent's garden shed where I began, but on where I would be in the future. So, when I took on my first commercial property, I already knew how I would lay it out and decorate it, which people would sit where and what they would be doing. In essence, I saw my whole company laid out like a reality, not a pipe-dream.

Think about visualisation in the same way you would think when you are about to go on a longed-for holiday. You concentrate on the beach you are going visit, that glass of chilled white wine, sleeping late and eating well. Your mind tells you to do this rather than dwelling on the possibility of a delayed and cramped flight or going back to work afterwards. You are focussing on the future positives, not the immediate negatives. It is very simple once you get the knack of it.

I decided to first build the right belief system and business model not only for my company but for customers, myself and the staff I would employ.

I knew if I focussed on building the right values for my company, it would work and when that happened, the money would follow.

Reaching an undeniable level of success will never protect you from the normal highs and lows of life, nor should it because that would not be natural. Even the Emperors of Ancient Rome had a servant whose job it was to whisper, "Remember you are only a man." But, as I have already mentioned, it does create some unique problems of its own. No one can always be on a high; that isn't realistic because life isn't perfect.

I believe I am fortunate in some ways because my lowest moments were at the beginning of my journey. From day one, despite hard times, I pushed until I had overcome my negativity and doubt. Eventually, I triumphed and have never looked back.

If you believe in yourself, have the necessary talent and act on those beliefs and talents, you can achieve any goal you choose. Though I am not suggesting you resort to crime, there is no right or wrong way to do it. It is about what's right for you. It is what you believe that's important. There are no set guidelines or ingredients for success.

There is a 16th-century terrestrial globe, The Hunt-Lenox Globe, in the New York Public Library, which shows what was then the extent of the charted world. Along the uncharted eastern coast of Asia is written the phrase, 'Here be dragons.' It was meant as a warning to explorers not to pass that point, and yet many did and discovered wondrous lands and made fortunes. Trust me when I tell you, there are no dragons. Just believe and take that first step.

As I said in the very first chapter, you don't land on a mountain; you climb a mountain. Every day will be a climb. Some days will be easy; some days will be tough.

Some days the climb is going to be so steep that you'll feel exhausted. You'll want to give up. But, if you quit, you'll spend the rest of your life wondering *what if?* If you believe you'll succeed, you will. If you believe you'll fail — you will. You must fight for what you believe in and keep on fighting. If you want to be a follower, someone else's employee all your life, that's OK. But I doubt you'd be reading this book if you did. If you see your peers climbing the ladder and leaving you behind, either in life or career, don't despair. Use that moment to pause and reassess. Take a hard look at why you feel like you're standing still.

Then, when you are ready, step out of your comfort zone and start climbing!

Within each of us lies the power to act: personally, professionally and emotionally. Never stop learning and never stop setting new goals.

I hope some of the lessons I've learned on the way will empower you on your journey.

If you think it will take luck instead of willingness, think about this:

- If you have luck, it won't help you unless you know what to do with it.

- If you get an opportunity, you need to know how to leverage off it.

- If you make money, you need to know how to spend wisely.

- If you have a dream, you need to know how to make it a reality.

I hope that, after reading this book, you will be both inspired and motivated to be the best you can be. And remember when you reach the edge of your known world, there are no dragons!

Now it is up to you to
WIN BIG AND RISK SMALL!'

www.ingramcontent.com/pod-product-compliance
Lightning Source LLC
Chambersburg PA
CBHW032104090426
42743CB00007B/230